Why settle for a slimy frog when you can have a real-life twenty-first-century prince who can answer your emotional, spiritual, and physical needs from the highest place, while adding an enchanting, unforgettable essence to your life?

Don't think you've got a frog habit? Check any of the following that apply:

- ❑ *I feel incomplete without a man or a relationship, so I partner quickly and it takes a long time for me to chuck bad relationships.*
- ❑ *I often date jerks because they're cute, successful, totally infatuated with me—or better than nothing.*
- ❑ *When I tell my female friends about the men in my life they are embarrassed for all of womankind.*
- ❑ *My male friends are embarrassed for all mankind.*
- ❑ *When I know the guy I'm seeing is a loser I'm more likely to scold myself for being too picky than I am to dump him.*

The more items you checked, the more likely you're a Frog Princess. Don't wait until you've had another weird date or lousy relationship to begin your recovery. With this indispensable handbook, you can start on the road to a frog-free life right now!

NAILAH SHAMI is the author of *Taking the High Road: How to Deal with Your Ex-Husband, Maintain Your Sanity, and Raise Your Child in Peace* (available from Plume). As the originator and director of National Get Along with Your Ex Month, she had been featured on CNN, Fox on Psychology, and several national radio programs, as well as in *USA Today*. She lives in the state of Washington.

Do Not Talk to, Touch, Marry, or Otherwise Fiddle with Frogs

HOW TO FIND
PRINCE CHARMING BY
FINDING YOURSELF

Nailah Shami

A PLUME BOOK

PLUME

Published by the Penguin Group
Penguin Putnam Inc., 375 Hudson Street,
New York, New York 10014, U.S.A.
Penguin Books Ltd, 27 Wrights Lane,
London W8 5TZ, England
Penguin Books Australia Ltd, Ringwood,
Victoria, Australia
Penguin Books Canada Ltd, 10 Alcorn Avenue,
Toronto, Ontario, Canada M4V 3B2
Penguin Books (N.Z.) Ltd, 182–190 Wairau Road,
Auckland 10, New Zealand

Penguin Books Ltd, Registered Offices:
Harmondsworth, Middlesex, England

First published by Plume,
a member of Penguin Putnam Inc.

First Printing, March 2001
10 9 8 7 6 5 4 3 2 1

 REGISTERED TRADEMARK—MARCA REGISTRADA

LIBRARY OF CONGRESS CATALOGING-IN-PUBLICATION DATA:
Shami, Nailah.
Do not talk to, touch, marry, or otherwise fiddle with frogs : how to find Prince
Charming by finding yourself / Nailah Shami.
p.   cm.
ISBN 0-452-28230-6
1. Love. 2. Man-woman relationships. I. Title.
BF575.L8 S552 2001
646.7'7—dc21   00-050185

Printed in the United States of America
Set in Futura Book
Designed by Leonard Telesca

BOOKS ARE AVAILABLE AT QUANTITY DISCOUNTS WHEN USED TO PROMOTE PRODUCTS OR
SERVICES. FOR INFORMATION PLEASE WRITE TO PREMIUM MARKETING DIVISION, PENGUIN
PUTNAM INC., 375 HUDSON STREET, NEW YORK, NEW YORK 10014.

To Imhotep,
The king of my heart
The gentle song in my soul.
The wind beneath my wings.
Thank you for your unwavering friendship, love, respect,
positivity, faith and constant comical commentary on a
lot of life's trials and tribulations that would have
driven most normal people to the living edge. And in case
I've never said it, I knew I loved you
before I met you too.
Tienes mi corazon, siempre.

CONTENTS

Do Not Talk to,
Touch, Marry, or
Otherwise
Fiddle
with Frogs

INTRODUCTION

Frogs Only Turn into Princes in Fairy Tales

What the fool does in the end, the wise man does in the beginning.
—Proverb

One rainy Saturday morning after reading an article in a magazine about the "10 Best Places to Pick Up Your Next Boyfriend and Make Him Instantly Fall for You," 32-year-old Jane doused herself with her newly arrived pheromone spray and bounced off to the grocery store to meet her next beloved. As she rounded the corner to the produce section she almost had a head-on cart collision with The One, who was plunking a bunch of bananas into his cart. Their eyes locked. She apologized for almost scrambling his eggs, giggled, quickly zoomed in on his empty ring finger and then asked him how he knew he'd gotten the best bunch. Scratching his chest in apelike fashion, he replied, "Oooh-oooh-oooh," like he'd spent more time in the jungle than Tarzan. Jane giggled again and asked him to pick a bunch for her, although bananas make her nauseous, and she really had no intention of buying anything other than another magazine if she didn't score in the produce section like the article promised. After exchanging names (his was Joe) and picking over the apples and pears, they rolled their carts side-by-side to the bakery to pick out a birthday cake for his sister's party. Soon enough, he asked for her number, promising to call her later that night after the party, and parted with another "Oooh-oooh-oooh."

"To the mall," Jane thought as she left the store, ignoring the clerk yelling after her about her abandoned bananas, "to buy a new outfit for our first date." Giddily, she called her mom from her car phone on the way to the mall to ask, "What did you wear on your first date with Dad?" But Joe didn't call that night like he promised, or the next. In fact, she didn't hear from him for a week, and when he called he didn't even have a vaguely creative excuse for his tardiness. Jane was somehow hoping to hear him say he washed the jeans he was wearing that day before emptying his pockets, and that it took a week of calling everyone with the 720 prefix to finally get to her. But he did ask her to dinner at her favorite Thai restaurant. During dinner the chemistry returned, but she could have sworn she saw him write his number down for the waitress when he signed for dinner. However, she didn't want to spoil the evening by busting him on the spot. They had a second date, and a third, and within a few months, she moved in with him. A year later, they married. A happily-ever-after story? It might have been, if not for Joe's advanced case of wandering-eyeitis, putdowns and slipshod fathering.

The wandering-eyeitis escalated after Jane gave birth to their son a year after their wedding. Instead of whiplash double-takes over strangers on the street, Joe was now ogling her friends, and once even stared just a little too long at her bikini-clad 17-year-old baby sister at a pool party. As fathering went, Joe was fair weather at best (when he was home). Diapers smelled too bad for him; the baby didn't come with a snooze button, and Jane, mind you, seemed too "distracted" with the baby around to dote on him. But what more could she have expected from a man who signed over his parenting rights to his 6-year-old son from his first marriage to his ex-wife's new husband in lieu of paying child support?

He was mean too. Upon returning to his castle after a late night at the office, the Frog Prince often asked sleek, size 8 Jane if she'd like to go for a run so she could burn off the baby fat. But then this was the same insensitive guy who told her before the nuptials that he didn't think he could love her if she swelled up like his porky ex-wife.

Jane knew Joe had major issues—character flaws, really—but perhaps she was still hopelessly under the spell of the pheromone spray and the Frog Prince fantasy, which as you might recall, went something like this:

> A fair young maiden was passing through the woods, marveling at the flowers, the singing birds, and the wonder of the day, when she happened upon a talking frog. A butt-ugly, bugeyed, green, fly-slurping thing he was, but nevertheless forward enough to say, "Kiss me and I will turn into a prince and we will live happily ever after." With visions of Antonio Banderas, castles, servants and a lifetime supply of blinding jewelry dancing in her head, the hopeful maiden closed her eyes and planted one on frog boy. And what do you know? He did turn into a prince. And they did marry, and live happily ever after. (Or so we were told. I suspect the new princess soon caught her prince slipping down to the pond for fly snacks and hopping all over the furniture—and do you think she ever really got over kissing Kermit?)

But back to Jane, who by and by discovered, as many frog-smitten women do, that outside of fairy-tale land, all the kisses, wishing, hoping, waiting and pretending in the world have yet to transform a frog—a man who Fails the Requirements Of Greatness—into a prince—a man who can Provide Romance,

Inspiration, Nurturing, and Character Easily and who Prevents Recurring, Idiotic, Negative, and Crazy Experiences. Instead of happily ever after, Jane got heartache ever after. After a few of Joe's affairs, *he* divorced her and she moved herself and her son in with her parents. Much to the dismay of her parents Jane recently started dating Benny, a married co-worker separated from his wife who occasionally drinks himself into a blackout. Croak.

Many women repeat foolish mating patterns like this, seemingly unable to inoculate themselves against frogs after first contact. How do we, who have dipped into the frog pond once, strengthen our psyches to the point that if we ever have another encounter of the froggy kind, cats will have learned to bark?

How do we fight the lonely night cravings after we've shooed away John and Joe Frog, or say "thanks-but-no-thanks" to the next cute bad boy who asks us out? How do we develop "prince" standards when we've never had them before?

Those were the questions that haunted me after I finished writing my first book, *Taking the High Road: How to Cope with your Ex-Husband, Maintain Your Sanity and Raise Your Child in Peace*—a survival and sanity guide for women who have to co-parent with a frog after a divorce or breakup. Men like Joe and my ex-husband, regretfully, were the warty stars of the show.

As I stepped back in time to trace my own footsteps along the frog recovery path—by this time wrapped in the richest love I could have ever imagined—a formula began to emerge:

$$\text{Self-love}^n - \text{frogs and bad mating habits}$$
$$+ \text{ healthy partnering strategies}$$
$$= \text{happily ever after}$$

Under the new model, we first love ourselves to the *nth* degree, boot all the frogs out of our lives, relinquish our old, unhealthy mating habits, and repair our hearts. Instead of reordering pheromone spray, we order a "Caribbean Cooking for One" video. Then one day if we bump into a man at the supermarket who looks a little like Michael Jordan deliberating over bananas, we get a good eyeful before brushing by to find a suitable mango for our Mango-Mint sauce. And so intent are we on getting the perfect one that we barely hear him ask us, twice, if we're enjoying the lovely weather. He flirts a little. We do too, and maybe even agree to go out on *one* date so we can take an honest, lingering look at him. If, after that, he appears to be a hop-along, we do not talk to, touch, marry or otherwise fiddle with him again. If we repeat this strategy, while building a delicious life that we enjoy, a prince will follow.

This formula worked for me after a yucky marriage and a string of dating disasters. I believe it can work for you too. What do you have to lose? Frogs, toads and tadpoles. What do you have to gain? Princes, self-respect, dignity and a healthy, honest, positive relationship with yourself.

It's taken me almost forty years to learn that there's a practical side to love and partnering. To discover that the man in my heart must not only exceed my romantic notions and eccentric tastes, but he must also wash the dishes, buy tampons, cook dinner, shop around for car insurance, help my daughter with algebra, know the difference between an asset and a liability, care for himself and come with his own joy. All the flirting, old-fashioned trickery, personal ads and pheromone sprays won't help you get a prince until in your soul, you finally, finally know the practical measure of love too.

So, we're going to take an adventurous yet grounded journey to relationship riches. If you're like Jane, or the way I used to be, on the following pages you will find an inspiring yet practical 12-step withdrawal and rediscovery handbook designed to help you release your craving for frogs and replace it with a generous helping of your own worth and power. From there, you can open your heart for more fulfilling relationships with men who are more like princes.

Choosing a mate is a big part of a warm, rich life, so why settle for a slimy frog when you can have a real-life twenty-first-century prince who can answer your emotional, spiritual and physical needs from the highest place, while adding an enchanting, unforgettable essence to your life?

The 12 Steps

You can walk for many miles, and yet no matter how much you try to do otherwise, you can only take one step at a time. Because you are tackling something monumental in this book, it's important that you go through it mindfully, conquering each step before you move to the next.

In Step 1, you will have an opportunity to review frogs past (and maybe present) for learning purposes and to begin the reclamation of your spirit.

In Step 2, you'll uncover the motivations behind your froggy interludes, and understand the connection between how you think, how you feel and how you behave.

In Steps 3 and 4, you'll generate a soul-stirring momentum for change, and begin the most important love affair of all—with yourself.

In Step 5, we'll cover frog recognition and weaning. If you've ever fallen head over heels for Brute, Boy-Boy or their froggy brethren, here you'll find the strength you need to wean yourself.

In Steps 6 and 7, you'll learn to replace limiting mating thoughts and patterns with empowering new mental attitudes and strategies, and permanently frog-proof yourself.

In Steps 8 and 9, you'll learn to adopt more discriminating standards for choosing men and apply them to new possibilities.

In Steps 10 and 11, as you discover how to find a prince without looking, you'll also explore methods to live juicy for two.

In Step 12, you'll review.

How to Use This Book

One day I was twenty minutes into a marathon race on the exercise bike at my health club, sweating like a hot pig, and a woman who was obviously new to the country (and exercise) plopped down on the bike next to mine. She put her feet on the pedals and just sat there, staring at me and then back at her blank monitor with puzzlement. "You have to turn it on and pedal," I said. "Oh," she said with a thick accent and pushed the "On" button and began to cycle. I reached over, still panting, and instructed her on how to select a fairly easy workout. Two minutes into her session, she smacked the "Off" button, retrieved a hoagie from the bottom of her gym bag and headed for the locker room. She came back days later and did exactly the same thing, and then I didn't see her again for months. The day she returned, I was on the treadmill. "You look so good," she said. "How do you look so good?" Panting and somewhat curious as to whether she had another hoagie in her gym bag, I promised to talk to her after I finished my run. When I shared my workout routine with her—three days of yoga a week, four days of aerobics, twenty minutes of weight training on alternate days—she flatly declared, "Too much work." Well, it was and it wasn't. This was no love affair. The gym was an acquired taste. Especially in the winter. If she only knew how many December and January mornings I had to coax myself out of the car when

I reached the gym. Because I was faithful, I got results. The same is true of my frog recovery. It's going to seem like a lot of work at first. And you're not going to want to do it some days.

But, if you want the lasting results this program can bring, you will have to show up and pedal too. And you will have to do it over and over again—without a cheerleader or any fanfare whatsoever, and with some occasional stalling, griping, and backpedaling—until you get what you want. As your fearless leader, I'll tell you instructional stories, pick your brain, challenge your old way of dating and then share new strategies with you for healthier relationships. The changework, however, is yours to do.

My next bit of advice is to take your time reading this book. It has taken you many years to create your partnering patterns. You will have to do more than spend a few hours speed-reading this book to learn to be smarter with your heart. Remember that these recovery steps are progressive, so master each one before moving on to the next. If you're willing to dedicate at least fifteen minutes a day to your recovery, you can permanently improve your mating habits.

Four Very Powerful Recovery Tools

Here are a few supportive, endurance-building tools that will help supplement your recovery process.

Affirmations

Hundreds of thousands of thoughts float through your mind each day and they create your behavior patterns. Some of these thoughts have led you to every frog you've ever known. For instance, if you constantly tell yourself that you aren't worthy of a prince, that you're getting too old to be so picky or that good men are hard to find, you will no doubt build a self-fulfilling prophecy and become a frog magnet. So be careful with your thoughts. If you want frogs out of your universe permanently, you will have to diligently change your thinking about men, relationships and, most important, yourself by changing your internal chatter.

Each step begins with three or four positive affirmations—short statements designed to flood your mind with upbeat, encouraging thoughts about yourself and healthy relationships. Recite each three times out loud, each day, in front of a mirror. Write your favorites on an index card and carry them in your purse or car, and whenever you feel your willpower slipping, repeat them throughout the day as many times as needed. You cannot o.d. on affirmations. While I withdrew from the second love of my life, I recited, "I am filled with power, wonder and strength" hundreds of times. I was shaky at first, very much wanting to shove aside my noble principles and my integrity for another moment in his arms, but by day's end, his pleading phone messages fell on deaf ears. If you've never used affirmations as a transformative tool, try not to be put off by a lack of sincerity when you first start. It's perfectly okay to fake it until you feel it. So, if you initially find yourself declaring "I am filled with power, wonder and strength" using the same hesitant tone with which you would say "I love liver and onions," stay with it. If you repeat these positive reminders anyway, your resistance will fall away and every day you will experience fewer negative, limiting thoughts.

R & R Journal

While you're reading this book, you're going to write one too—your R&R Journal. The first "R" is for "recovery" and the

second is for "rapture." You're going to use both of these con-
cepts simultaneously to re-create your mating style, and this is
where you'll record your results. By putting your transitional
thoughts and experiences down in a hardbound or spiral journal, you will get in touch with revealing patterns and insights. If
you've been mixed up with frogs for a long time, or with a single frog who seemed like ten rolled into one, your R & R journal
will quickly become an essential partner in healing your misguided
psyche. As you write you will discover many things—your motivations, stumbling blocks and inner rhythm. I encourage you to
not only write about your pride at how well you are doing, and
the positive baby steps you make, but also to write about your
fears and doubts. Don't be surprised if you pen an account of
your triumphant breakup with a frog one night and your burning midnight craving for him the next. Write about things that
please you. Write about things that don't. Write whether you
think it's recovery-related or constructive. Our subconscious
minds make lopsided connections sometimes. Everything you
write is right.

At the end of each step, you will find at least one R&R Journal writing theme, but you should also write about one of the
topics in Ninety-Nine Recovery & Rapture Journal Ideas (on
page 221) once a day. For best results, always write what is on
the tip of your mind, write the truth and *write your heart*. Even if
it's simply a string of unrelated words, like "yippee!" "Yuck"
"yellow" and "yard sale." On occasion, I have filled pages with
the words "I'm still here." In her book *The Artist's Way*, Julia
Cameron suggests writing first thing in the morning, before
your inner critic is fully awake. Don't worry about spelling,
punctuation, grammar or style. Even if you think it's gobbedly-
gook, just keep writing, and you will see over time what an important biofeedback and transformational tool it can be—like

self-portraits of you at any given moment in time—that can help you get in touch with the real you and meet her needs and ultimately transport you to the life you want to create.

Prince Cameos

Frogs get good PR. This month, I've heard three froggy news stories already. One frog gambled away his wife's inheritance. Another got his driver's license suspended for having too many DWIs, and the third confessed to a year-long affair with his assistant. I also overheard two "girlfriend grapevine reports" last week at the beauty salon. One woman said her sister's husband slept with her best friend. The other's boyfriend had slapped her the night before (and it wasn't the first time). Coupled with your own frog mini-sagas, other froggy tales can often make princes start to seem more and more like urban legends.

But you know what? Most of the men on the planet don't gamble away inheritances (or hard-earned savings), or drive while under the influence of drugs or alcohol, or have a romp in the hay with their beloved's best friend. They are decent, good, sweet souls who've dwelled on the meaning of integrity, character and love for a long, long time. It would tickle me no end to see a reporter stick a mike in the face of some father who's taking his child to the park or grocery shopping for his family to ask him what his motives were.

I stuck a virtual mike in the faces of twelve women who love princes and asked them that question, and their answers appear throughout the book in the form of Prince Cameos. Most princes put their pants on one leg at a time and probably leave the toilet seats up (I didn't ask). They don't slay dragons or live in castles, and they often work in the background, shuttling their kids to school, making peanut butter and jelly sandwiches, and mowing your mother's lawn. The late Mother Teresa would have said of them, "They do ordinary things with great care." And yet, they have a certain presence, genuineness, an endearing spark. *They simply shine.*

As you read about these husbands, fathers, friends and lovers, you'll be installing healthy "prince flash cards" in your mind. Your faith in princes will grow and you will start to gravitate toward men with honorable motives who will take care of your heart.

Listen to what their honeys say about them. Most women who have successful ten- or twenty-five-year relationships don't fixate on the things most women who choose frogs do. They don't say, "I wish he had been cuter, or richer or Italian." They say, "I like the way he always brings a steaming mug of hot chocolate to the bed for me on those cold winter mornings." Or "I was half crazy nursing the baby every other hour last night and he woke up every time to rub my back and tell me how much he loved me." They say things like "He shaved his head when I went through chemotherapy," or "Although he was broken and destroyed too when our daughter died, he kept me sane and helped me when I didn't want to move anymore," or "He comes home every day and before he takes the trash out or plops down on the couch, he finds me wherever I am in the house and kisses me, and then he plays with our boys."

Make prince sightings a daily practice in your own life. Count the number of times men hold doors open for you, pass parking spots because they see you behind them, compliment your hair even when you think you look like Raggedy Ann, and smile at you without hounding you for your phone number. The princes shouldn't have to make up for the frogs, but they do. *Celebrate them.*

Recovery Exercises

A former college professor, who my fellow students and I all thought was in the early stages of Alzheimer's because he kept repeating the same points over and over like it was the first time, told us this while he was passing out our final grades. "What you don't say over and over, people forget. So, I kept saying what was important over and over and over, so you would remember." I'm going to do the same thing, so bear with me. It's my job to make sure you get this right so you can go where the love is and create healthier relationships. The reminders at the end of each section will also sum up key points of that step to further help you soak up the lessons, and the exercises will help you apply them in your life.

What I Wish for You

Because this is a recovery process and a vision quest, you're going to learn a lot more about yourself in the coming pages than you may have planned on. "Stuff" is going to come up. And that stuff may be surprising, painful and awkward. So much so that you want to run from it, suppress it or scurry back to hide out in frog land. Forget about horror movies, sometimes there is nothing scarier than going back to face the you you used to be.

In a few moments, you're going to begin a dynamic and comprehensive healing process filled with lessons in self-mastery, self-love, empowerment and grace to help you establish winning mating strategies. When you're finished, you will not be the same woman. The vision I held of you while writing this book is that you are someone who wants to make the changes necessary to create healthy mating strategies. By the time you finish this book I hope you would no more share your love or your life with a frog than you would reach for a pair of rusty pliers to yank out your wisdom teeth. If you keep these five core thoughts with you while you read, they will help alleviate any discomfort that arises.

1. You don't have to kiss a lot of frogs to get to your prince, but you do have to stop kissing frogs.
2. If you want a better quality man, you have to take more care choosing him.
3. If you want to change your limiting behavior, change your thoughts.
4. If you develop an endless fascination with yourself, self-control, self-respect, and integrity, a prince will follow.
5. Life is easier—love is easier—when you make good mate choices.

When you choose a prince, love can be both a sacred sanctuary and a magical journey. That's what I have now, and that is what I wish for you.

STEP 1

Fess Up to Your Frog Addiction

Lesson: To create better mating habits, first you have to admit you have a problem, and get nose-to-nose with it in the privacy of your own heart. As you journey back to your "first contact" and two other major froggy relationships, you'll learn the lessons, forgive yourself and begin to prepare for healthier behavior.

Affirmations

1. I am a woman of power, wonder and strength.
2. Admitting I have a frog challenge is the first step in my recovery.
3. Today, I release all ancient dating habits and I forgive myself completely for any unhealthy relationships I've had.

Knowing I would have to admit I used to have a frog habit was the hardest part of deciding to write this book. Last night, in fact, I dreamt that I was up at the podium at a Frogs Anonymous meeting, hunched over ever so slightly, mumbling, "Hi, my name is Nailah and I used to be a Frog Princess." A short woman in the first row gasped and said, "Girl, what did you say?" And I ran off the stage, hysterical because I couldn't bear to repeat myself. And now as I sit here, I'd still rather not, but it's true. I *was* a Frog Princess. The quicker you fess up too, the quicker you can change.

What Is a Frog, and Why They Belong on Lily Pads, Not in Your Living Room

Last year when I asked about a hundred women—many of them recovering from nasty divorces—to share their prince wish lists with me, "sensitive," "faithful," "romantic," "responsible" and "loving" topped the list. In a side-by-side feature comparison, a "frog" list would look like a game of negative word association, featuring antonyms like: "brutish," "unfaithful," "crude," "immature" and "cold."

The nature of frogs is actually that simple. Think of everything you want in a prince and then imagine the anti-prince showing up to invoke the kind of drama, heartache and disappointment that would have the writers of The Young and the Restless beating down your door for script material. Frogs are unfit for cohabitation or cuddling with you, your best friend, your sister or any woman looking for a positive, healthy relationship. If your own froggy interludes have not proven this to you, then check out this froggy sextet:

⤞ BOBBY, 39, has had three restraining orders served on him in the last year: one from his ex-wife, one from his ex-father-in-law, and one from a girlfriend he pushed out of his car after a dance one night, leaving her stranded at a club at 1:30 A.M. since she didn't want to have sex with him because she was on her period. "If you can dance you can screw!" he yelled as he sped off.

❧ JOEL married a woman with two children. Then, two years later, he moved back home with his mother (at age 42), claiming the kids were too much trouble. He got his way when his wife dropped her daughters off at her sister's and moved in with Joel and his mom.

❧ PAUL, 42, has been married three times, and always has, as he says, "a chick on the side. Most women can't keep up with my sex drive. I need it at least two times a day, every day."

❧ TONY, 28, a salesman, has been fired from several jobs for bizarre behavior and inconsistent performance. One week, he's at the top of his game, outselling everyone in the district. The next, he's the sullen, closed-door office hermit who drinks his lunch at a local bar.

❧ KEN, 25, is still looking for a woman who wants to be barefoot and pregnant, seen and not heard, and will not question anything he says or does. He recently answered an ad offering mail-order brides.

❧ REX, 29, is a cold fish who prefers straight missionary sex with all the lights out and thinks cuddling is for sissies. "The only time I touch a woman is when I'm having sex with her. Afterwards, I either get up and take a shower, or roll over and go to sleep. I prefer prostitutes, but I'm afraid of getting AIDS."

Now tell me, would you want to spend all of eternity with any of these men?

We've Become Desensitized to Frogs

Anyone who's watched half a dozen scary movies knows it takes a little more gore the next time to make our skin crawl. A mere head being cut off is nothing if you watch *Tales from the Crypt* night after night after night. Unfortunately, the same type of desensitization can rear its ugly head in the dating world. Thirty-five-year-old Charlotte, for example, is on her fifth "married-wink-separated" man. "I know he's going to get a divorce soon. They're just working out the details. Isn't love about patience?" In other words, she has developed a tolerance for married men. Some of you may have one for cheaters, alcoholics, bruisers or one of the other frog varieties we'll be reviewing in Step 5.

What you come to expect and accept in men is exactly what you will get. Twenty-four-year-old Maya has been living with a guy who hasn't spoken to her for a month because she cut her hair. Everybody loves it except him, but the real point is it's *her* hair, and no grown man should start a cold war over the length of the hair on his beloved's head. Before him, she dated another passive-aggressive semi-mute who once washed two of her favorite dry-clean-only silk blouses with Tide after a spat.

The longer the froggy relationship or the more exposure you have to frogs, the more habit-forming they can become and the greater your tolerance grows. One afternoon I sat with a new friend who was pouring out the sorry details of her ten-year marriage and she told me two things I didn't know about her husband—that he smoked marijuana three to four times a week and rarely came home before 2 A.M. on the weekends. I sat there dumbstruck and then I asked, "How long has this been going on?" "For the past four years," she said. "Right after Josh was born."

A lot of women I interviewed also developed frog habits through:

❧ *Hypnosis.* Cute, sexy and charming frogs are master hypnotists. Whereas the frog in the Frog Princess fairy tale was green and slimy with bulging eyeballs, many modern frogmen come cloaked in heavenly bodies with silky voices and soft doe eyes. A friend proudly denounced all ugly-acting Pretty Boys over lunch one day. And yet when the phone rang about fifteen minutes later, she spotted her old Tom Cruise lookalike boyfriend's number on the caller ID—her ugly-acting Tom Cruise lookalike boyfriend—and picked up the phone and told him she was over him, *and then* she asked him if he was over her yet. After a bit of his typical whispery hypnotic cooing, she was entranced and strolled out on her patio with the cordless while I sat there debating whether or not to run after her and throw my glass of water on her to break his hypnotic lock.

❧ *Denial.* In the name of research, not long after my initial interview with many of the Frog Princesses whose stories appear in this book, I called them up and pretended to recite someone else's frog list to them—but it was actually a list of things they had earlier reported not liking about their current or last husband or boyfriend— and then I asked them if they would ever date someone like that. The ones who didn't say "no," said "Hell no." That sneaky little exercise convinced me that a lot of women are Queens of Denial when it comes to an honest assessment of their own love partners.

❧ *Grand Ms. Fix-it Delusions.* Some women like putting things together, polishing them up, decorating them, or converting some raggedy throwaway into something else they want. As one girlfriend who quilts put it, "I used to think I could do the same thing with men that I do with my quilt squares. Take a bit of this, a bit of that, add a background and a border and sew it all together into a work of art. I've learned not to patch together anything that walks and talks and has a mind of its own anymore."

❧ *Faulty Pride.* Fear of being "outed" as a Frog Princess or being labeled the family leper has stopped many a woman from dumping a frog. It took 39-year-old Felecia, who recently became the first divorcée in her family, five years to work up the courage to shove her pride aside and share the following confession with her family last Christmas, "He's been unfaithful three times and he's going to have a baby in a few months with the last one."

❧ *Redeeming Quality Rebates.* Have you ever let a frog's redeeming qualities overshadow fatal flaws? Like overlooking his "droopy butt" jokes about you because he makes a lot of money or is good in bed? "Last year I told my mom I was going to visit a jailbird I'd been writing for two months," said 30-year-old Song. "I told her he'd embezzled some money and he had a couple more years to serve, but he still seemed like my soul mate in his letters. Then I rolled out my sell list: He sends me thoughtful scented notes, says he still owns a big house in Denver and he speaks French."

❧ *Not Knowing the Difference Between a Good Man Who's Having a Bad Moment, and a Green-blooded Frog.* Every man has a bad moment once in a while. Frogmen, on the other hand, hop from one bad moment to the next. After noticing a strange recurring number on his pager for weeks, 22-year-old Mandy parked her car a block away from her boyfriend's home at 6:00 one morning, crawled across his wet lawn to his bedroom window and caught him asleep in bed with another woman. They made up after he explained that he loved her but he had a sex addiction and was seeing a counselor. A month later, she caught him tonguing another woman at a nightclub. For future reference, here's a handy chart that will help you distinguish between a good man having a bad moment and a frog:

Good Man, Bad Moment	**Frog**
Does an occasional, sly double take when he sees an attractive woman.	Passes out his pager number to attractive women.
Is somewhat grumpy on Monday mornings.	Calls you a bitch for using his hairbrush one morning.
Fibbed about the number of girlfriends he had before you.	Never told you he was still married to a woman in another state after five months of dating you.
Gets a little testy the fifth time you ask for his opinion of the new dress he's already convincingly praised with, "You look great, babe."	Slaps you because you bought a new dress.
You came home early from a business trip to find a ton of dishes piled in the sink.	You came home early from a business trip to find your man and your so-called best friend piled up in your bed.

Good Man, Bad Moment	*Frog*
Yells at the kids for fighting in the house.	Was logged onto an Internet porn chat room while the kids were fighting in the house.
Didn't clean up the mess he and his poker buddies left in the den one night.	Tells your 16-year-old daughter and her friends they can have the leftover beers after his poker game.

Ten Sure Signs You've Got a Frog Habit

So, you're a few pages in and perhaps you're thinking you're not a Frog Princess after all. You didn't try to massage one of the froggy sextet into a good catch a few pages ago. You've never had a prison pen pal, and no man has ever slapped you. Just a few bad men, a few bad moments, but still within the range of allowable relationship bloopers.

It's best to authentically pinpoint your own truth instead of having someone call you on it—especially not a sneaky little Down-with-Frogs Evangelist like me, so I'm going to let you take a closer look at what your choice in men really says about you. On your best Girl Scout honor, put checks in all of the boxes below that are true.

❑ I feel incomplete without a man or a relationship so I partner quickly, and it takes a long time for me to chuck bad relationships.

❑ I often date jerks because they're cute, successful, totally infatuated with me or better than nothing.

❑ If a man has money, I'm more likely to overlook character flaws.

❑ I feel bad, stupid or disappointed in myself after hooking up with a lot of the men in my life.

❑ According to my closest friends, my last love interest sucked.

❑ The three before them sucked too.

❑ When I tell my female friends about the men in my life they are embarrassed for all of womankind.

❑ My male friends are embarrassed for all mankind.

❑ My love life has had more dramatic twists and turns than *All My Children*.

❑ I'm more likely to scold myself for being too picky when I know the guy I'm seeing is a loser, than I am to dump him.

The more items you checked, the greater your frog magnet potential, and the more work you're going to have to do to adopt healthier dating habits so you won't be a Frog Princess anymore. Don't wait until you've had another questionable or sour date or relationship to begin your recovery.

Scared Straight: A Stephen King Preview of Your Future If You Don't Change Your Froggy Ways

Not long after I saw my first live pig, I stopped eating pork. I was only nine or ten, but when I saw what they looked like up close, how they smelled and what they ate, I became semi-hysterical and began boycotting the sausage links my mom put on my plate. In my little wild mind I had soundly concluded that if I kept eating big, smelly, snouty, slop-guzzling creatures I'd be full of slop, and that maybe I'd even start grunting and oinking and swell up. To this day, the sight of ham chunks and bacon bits at a salad bar still evokes an image of my head on a pig's body.

I had many similar queasy inner conflicts the last two years of my first marriage that my psyche couldn't reconcile either. Why was I, a financially and spiritually evolving health food enthusiast, sharing a refrigerator with a man who snacked on pork hotlinks, smoked a pack of unfiltered Camels a day, frequently drained our savings for carpe diem ventures and nighttime fun and was ever fond of remarking that "God" spelled backwards was "dog"?

Sometimes you don't remember the exact moment of a scared-straight epiphany, but as sure as I recall the lasting image that spurred my pork retreat, I clearly recall the day I knew for sure that Smokey the Bear had to go. It was my 29th birthday and as usual, I was celebrating up a storm. I wore a bouquet of purple flowers on my wrist, and a friend hired a purple wizard to serenade me with the "Happy Birthday" song in my office.

When I arrived home, still full of birthday glow, I gathered my curious daughter on my lap and answered her zillion questions about my day. And then her dad, who had been slumped on the couch glaring at the TV, looked up eventually and said, "I still can't believe you celebrate your birthday like a five-year-old."

As I slowly squared my eyes on the grinch who was trying to steal my birthday by poking fun at the way I celebrate one of my favorite days of the year, I realized for the first time in our married life that he either didn't have a clue who I was, or he knew and didn't approve. It's not as if I was doing anything unusual. He'd seen me order a bunch of balloons on a grocery shopping trip because it was the first Tuesday of the month and then tie them to my wrist after we paid for them; go to work for Halloween dressed up like a Christmas tree; and most days when we were out in public together he knew he could count on at least three people asking me where I was from because I rarely wore anything that looked vaguely like what he called "normal American people clothing." Who was this man and what had he done with my husband?

Later that night, and the next few nights, I slipped into a vision quest, which spanned our marital past, present and future. I solemnly and silently went over every detail of our relationship. First, I looked at its face value like a logical scientist, and then, like with the pork thing, I blew everything grossly out of proportion in Stephen King style. My theme? The Worst Things That Could Happen to Me as His Wife for the Next Ten Years. I saw him feeding my daughter, Esprit, pork rinds and hotlinks. I saw him flicking cigarette ashes into my carrot juice and refusing to go outside to smoke anymore, and both Esprit and me getting sick from his second-hand smoke. I saw myself with rotted brown teeth and bird's nest hair as we moved our cardboard home from one street corner to the next. I saw him staging gloom-and-doom Black Death birthday parties for me, and toasting me at my fortieth birthday with pork blood.

When I was finished with my haunting premonitions, and more than a little scared straight, the next time I looked at him, I felt like I'd woken up with amnesia and someone pointed to him and said, "And this is your husband. It may take some time to get used to being with him again, but in time your memory will return and you can go back to the life you had together." Although I carefully spent another thousand hours considering all the reasons I married him, and how I could make do, it was never the same again. And it didn't take long before I suddenly felt a hundred times dumber than dirt about my choice of husbands than I felt when I shaved my unruly eyebrows off at 14 and redrew them in with eyeliner for a whole year until they grew back in.

Have you ever envisioned your future with a frog, with a heavy emphasis on the morbid and macabre? It's not pretty stuff. Nothing like the kind of warm fuzzies you get watching *Touched by an Angel* or old reruns of *The Waltons*. But it may be just what you need right now to kick off your pilgrimage to the land of princes and honey.

We're going to start your scared straight mini-movie in a minute, but first I'd like you to take a few deep breaths and allow your body to relax. Put your hand on your heart, close your eyes, and allow yourself to imagine your last frog (or your current one) in your mind's eye standing in front of you. Study his face, his hands, and his whole body as if you'd just been commissioned to paint it on canvas. Now hear his voice, perhaps replaying the last thing he said to you, noting the tone and cadence. Then think about the way you feel around him, and some of the most unpleasant moments you've shared with him. Now, imagine that something a hundred times worse could happen next week—that your worst fear or the thing about him that disgusts you most could suddenly unfold. It doesn't matter if it will or not. Just imagine that it might. Next, bring to mind one trait or physical habit of his that gets on your last nerve and magnify it until you don't think you'll ever be able to sit in a room with him again without throwing up. Put yourself completely in each of these visualizations by bringing in all your senses of sight, sound, touch, taste and feeling. Over-embellish. Get a little hysterical (if you do this when you're close to getting your period, you'll do better at this exercise). Then go a year into the future, and then three years into the future to update your movie. And when you're finished open your eyes and write essay answers to the following questions in your R & R Journal.

1. What's the worst thing that can happen to my mind if I stay with this man for the next year? The next three years?
2. What's the worst thing that can happen to my heart if I stay with this man for the next year? The next three years?

3. What's the worst thing that can happen to my body if I stay with this man for the next year? The next three years?
4. What's the worst thing that can happen to my spirit if I stay with this man for the next year? The next three years?
5. What will I miss if he's in my life?
6. Who will I lose if I stay with him?
7. Which trait of his is most likely to eventually drive me absolutely, totally nuts?
8. If I don't already have a child with him, what would scare me the most about having one with him? If I do have one with him, what scares me the most about parenting with him?

If your own answers weren't enough to scare you straight, then picture yourself in the shoes of one of the women from the Frog Catcher's Hall of Shame.

Frog Catcher's Hall of Shame

✒ *Cheryl, 27, administrative assistant.* "I was in a two-year relationship with a man I knew had fidelity issues because he slept with me while he had another steady girlfriend. He ended up cheating on me in the end with his boss who is ten years older than him."

✒ *Sage, 25, software engineer.* When her fiancé broke off their engagement to chase after his high-school sweetheart, Sage begged him back with flowers and gifts, and promised not to whine or put up a fuss when he said he wanted to have a once-a-week movie night with his old honey. Sage has just been diagnosed with clinical depression.

❧ ***Reyna, 27, florist.*** In the two years she's been married, her 40-year-old husband has run home to his parents' house seven times after spats over housework and bills. Seven times, she's gone to get him.

❧ ***Meg, 29, dentist.*** Turning a blind eye to his gambling addiction, Meg married the one and only guy she had ever dated at 22. He had a good, high-powered job, but his excessive gambling exhausted their life savings and now they call a low-rent-district apartment home.

❧ ***Lynda, 45, biologist.*** "Once I was so infatuated with a married writer friend that I entrapped him into having sex with me," says Lynda. "Ironically, I got the hots for him after I saw how wonderful and attentive he was with his wife and two girls, and I wanted that in my life too. I began asking him over to fix things, always dressed in the skimpiest thing I had. He weakened one night after a little wine and we had sex. His wife found out and divorced him. We're together, but not like they had it. Sometimes he looks at me like I cost him his family."

❧ ***Janet, 41, attorney.*** Janet was married for seven years to an alcoholic who cheated on her with her neighbor for several years. During his secret love affair, Janet tried everything from Wonderbras to liposuction to regain his waning attention. When she learned of the affair, in his defense, he said, "I couldn't help myself, you know I'm compulsive. I didn't tell you because I didn't want to hurt you."

Finally, from the Land of Double Shame

❧ ***Bree, 42, travel agent.*** This divorced mother of two teenage boys met a dashing local actor who told her he was sort of still married (but only because his wife refused to sign the divorce papers). She moved him into her house the same month. He didn't have a job because he wanted to be available for an audition if his agent called. He was short-tempered with her boys, mooched a car and expense money out of her and lo and behold, when a concerned friend of hers did some snooping at the courthouse, he learned that her Romeo had applied for four marriage licenses with other women in the past year. Nevertheless, she went on to have two babies with him.

 Martha, 46, was a mistress to a guy who'd been saying he was going to get divorced for three years. His wife became pregnant with their second child last week. "Well I couldn't let her know I was going to leave her. She would have taken me to the cleaners," he told Martha.

Anything sound familiar? Does that scare you straight? Good. Now, it's time to saunter through your own Hall of Shame.

Remembering First, Second and Third Contact

Okay, now that you've seen the Hall of Shame, it's time to take a good look at what you've been dragging home. In your R&R Journal, write a short, narrative blurb about your first, second and third contact with frogs which includes his name, the nature of your relationship with him, your age or mental state, his good and bad traits, and your most memorable moment with him.

As an example, here are my first, second and third contacts:

1. I dated Frog 1, a chain-smoking artist who ate pork, when I was 17 because I thought he was cute, charming and creative. At 24, I married him and it lasted almost eight years. We had a daughter who continues to sprinkle my life with stardust.

2. I dated Frog 2, a mysterious inventor, overseas during a two-year breakup with Frog 1 prior to our marriage, because I thought he was suave, outrageously funny and worshipped the ground I ran on. And after a year of enchantment, he hopped on a plane to take care of some business in the States and I found out, via his wife one week later, that he had returned to her and the son he'd abandoned. Who knew? Her letter explained how he'd spilled his guts about "us," and she'd forgiven him and granted her permission to end it, and accused me of being a wannabe homewrecker.

3. I dated Frog 3 when I was bored because he was a creative, spiritual, adventurous businessman, though it seemed that every time we had a chat about the future of our relationship, a natural disaster occurred or he became ill. His kitchen caught on fire; a tree fell on his car; he tripped over a dog bone, sprained his ankle, and developed a curiously adaptive flu bug. He broke up with me—thank you, God—to move his company to another state.

Your True Confession

The first step in your recovery is to be honest enough with yourself to throw up your hands and confess to your frog-catching ways. What you cannot claim, you cannot conquer. Fib to your girlfriends, your family, your neighbors and your co-workers; lie on the questionnaire you just filled out; but skip the snow job on yourself. You deserve the very best and knowing you haven't had it is the first step to turning things around. If you had to put your hand on the Bible right now, or swear on your favorite tube of lipstick, or get up in front of a council of recovered frog addicts and say you'd dashed across the Freeway of Life without so much as one frog print on your back, would you choke on your tongue? Then it's time to fess up.

I want you to write today's date and your true confession in your R&R Journal. It could be as short and simple as, "I have failed to honor myself by choosing good men."

Now, for the good news. Whatever you just wrote in your R&R Journal is history, it's curable and you can start changing your froggy patterns today.

Taking Back Your Heart

A froggy touch can echo in your life for a long, long time after you've gotten rid of the frog, a lot like childhood scars and stretch marks. Kyla puts it like this, "I know it's silly, but every time my ex comes to pick our daughter up for his weekends, I find myself trying to figure out what I could have done to keep him from leaving me and whether the next man I love will throw me away too."

If you're still running around with a bruised ego, self-loathing, a raunchy man-hating attitude, or other frog baggage strapped to your back, then a piece of your heart is still with him. Maybe even a piece of your soul. And I believe you need all the pieces of you that you can hold on to to do the good stuff you came here for. When I finally quit pounding on myself for my marital slip, I had more brain time to ponder the magic of compound interest and the stock market, how long it would take me to put two layers of scented body cream all over my body twice a day, or finding the lowest airfares on the web so I could really see if the rain in Spain falls mainly on the plains.

If you want to resolve negative feelings about old loves and the self-badgering that often goes hand in hand with them, try this 3-step formula:

❧ *Forgive.* To permanently evict froggy ghosts from your psyche, you must forgive them, and then forgive yourself. Breathe. You can do this. One of the keys to forgiveness is knowing that it is a largely selfish act to help you heal wounds, and make *yourself* stronger and better. Once you forgive, the pieces of your heart and your soul that you've leased out to frogs will come flooding back to you.

The best way to forgive is to glean the lessons and then find a way to be grateful for them. Don't choke. Just sit with that notion for a few seconds, and then go get a glass of water if you need to. What I want you to do now is whisper the name of the frog who'd be hardest to forgive right now. Yes, the big croak.

Now create a list of five to ten reasons you think he's the big croak and put it to the side. We'll call this List A. Now create a list of five to ten positive things he taught you (List B). If something comes out negative the first time, write it down, and then work with it until it looks more like a blessing. For instance, if you write, "I learned not to trust men because they all cheat," cross it out and beside it write something positive, like "I learned to find men I can trust" or "I learned to take better care of myself." Next, complete this statement for each item on your list. "I forgive (his name) for (item from List A). From this I learned (your blessing from List B) and I'm so grateful." Do this for each guy you've got unresolved issues with, and then do it for each of the unsettled feelings you have about yourself. It's probably not going to take the first time, so repeat this exercise whenever you need to.

🐸 *Release.* In your mind, sit across from Frog 1 in the exercise above with your fill-in-the-blank forgiveness statements from a moment ago. Then, read each item to him, and as you do, picture him slowly vaporizing with each word. Repeat this process for each frog you want to release now and then burn the list and wash your hands.

🐸 *Replenish.* Imagine your heart opening up like a rose in bloom. Then picture itsy, bitsy symbolic icons of each of the things you love tenderly floating into your heart flower. Feel the warmth and the joy they bring you as they settle into your heart center. Coo if you want to. Then put your hand on your heart and seal this moment with the words "I love you (your name)."

Your Frog Fast

You cannot lose weight if you keep stuffing pizza in your mouth. You cannot develop healthy mating habits if you keep gobbling up frogs. So, for the duration of this book (and hopefully forever) you're going on a frog fast. What that means is:

1. No frogs for breakfast.
2. No frogs for lunch.
3. No frogs for dinner.
4. No frog snacks.
5. No frogs, period.

I'm going to load you up with tons of weaning techniques in Step 5, but for now, I just want you to trust me and make a basic commitment now to give yourself the time to recover without froggy interference. This pledge will work better if you keep it close to your heart and only share it with a few people who you know will support you, if anyone. If this is your book, please sign the contract below as your recovery pledge to me and yourself, complete your recovery exercises, read about Prince Daniel and meet me in Step 2.

I _____ am, or I am becoming, a wonder in the world. I believe in the spirit of my heart enough to know that I deserve a man of substance and quality, my prince.

I will not be shaken from this notion by frogs or duped into unhealthy relationships by loneliness, lust or desperation.

Neither will I be talked down by cynical spinsters or Frog Princesses who have given up on healthy, loving relationships.

I will learn to cherish myself completely before I go looking for my next love. And I will hold on and hold out until I have a prince. I swear.

_____

Date _____

Recovery Exercises

1. If you're currently involved with a frog, force yourself to recite the worst parts of that relationship several times a day in front of the mirror, and when you're finished say this, "I am now willing to invest in my healing so I can create something better."

2. Put together a small Frog album that contains a picture of each of the frogs you've dated and a short synopsis of what you learned from each of them. (Use List B if you like.) Then practice forgiving them.

R & R Journal exercise: Finish this thought with a page in your R & R Journal. "I developed my frog habit by . . ."

Prince Daniel

Daniel, a 25-year-old photographer, didn't want children because he wanted to travel the world. But when his longtime girl-friend announced she was pregnant and wanted to give the baby up for adoption, his paternal instincts kicked in. Two hours before they were scheduled to sign the adoption papers, he called it off and is now raising his 3-year-old daughter Kenya alone. His mother tells the rest of the story.

I raised Daniel and his three brothers as a single mother, and when they were growing up, single fathers were almost unheard of. But there was one with two daughters who attended my church. He was a kind, loving, gentle father who openly adored his girls and put their needs first. My son Daniel reminds me a lot of him.

When you see Daniel with Kenya, you'd never know he never wanted children because he treats her like she's the prize of all prizes and he plans his life around her. For him, coloring and cooking come before clubbing and chasing women like most of his friends do. Sometimes I offer to baby-sit so he can go out and dance like he used to when he was childless, but he'd rather spend his nights with Kenya. "She needs me here," he says.

For the first six months of her life, he lived off his savings so he could be at home with her. He changed diapers; comforted her through teething, ear infections; sang her lullabies— the works. Sometimes he just sat holding her while she slept. Now, she's in daycare for half a day four days a week so he can earn a living, but it took him months to find a daycare that was just right for her, so he only worked on the weekends, when his aunt or I could baby-sit. And then he felt guilty when he worked twelve-hour days to make up for the income he missed during the week.

In my first Mother's Day card from him after Kenya was born, he wrote, "I want to stay close to her and give her my very best as often as I can, like you did for me."

STEP 2

Find Out What's at the Root of Your Froggy Picks

Lesson: This step will help you determine the self-defeating triggers, fatal fantasies and other background mating rituals behind your froggy picks so you can overcome them.

Affirmations

1. I am willing to pay more attention to my mating habits.
2. I enjoy having healthy relationship fantasies.
3. I'm turning my weaknesses into strengths.

When my friends and I heard that one of our college girl-friends was going to cart off all of her belongings to her new love nest with one of our married professors, five of us staged a "Girl, Have You Lost Your Mind?" intervention. We brought teddy bears, a vibrator, hugs, and played girl power records, but she blocked us out with her ready mantra, "When I look into those cinnamon eyes, I want him, I want him, I want him." After three hours, we sadly concluded that she was too far gone, said a few prayers over her and marched out of the room.

Last night, I thought of her again when I saw an over-dramatic actress in a comical remake of *Dracula* bum rush her protective sister and flee from her home to rendezvous with Count Dracula. After tackling her sister and jumping off the veranda, she even said, "But he has bound me to his will with his eyes, I must go to him."

Let's face it, if we were in our right minds, we would say little more than "ugh" if a blood-sucking vampire or a fly-slurping frog threw himself in front of us, but strong triggers and hopeful fantasies can turn healthy relationship ideals into mush. The more aware you are of them, the more you can ward off Frog Mind—a state of thinking that puts you at risk of being smitten by a frog.

Healthy Dating Requires Attention

There are two things I always want to ask women when I hear them whining about a bad relationship and then pleading ignorance about how it started:

1. When are you going to call the producers of *The X-Files* and tell them you're some amorous body snatcher's favorite victim, so they can base a story on you?
2. If you're not some amorous body snatcher's favorite victim, tell me how you think you ended up with your last frog?

Most of the feedback I hear from question 2 has me convinced that they've put a whole new twist on the concept of blind dating. For the record, a blind date is going out for a social get together with someone you don't know on a friend or family member's recommendation. *It is not* keeping your eyes shut while you're dating and then acting surprised when you pop them open one day and there before you stands the Frog Wonder.

Take 33-year-old Connie for example, who spun this hapless tale for me of how she launched an eight-month live-in relationship with Ian the moocher playboy. "He started e-mailing me very intensely for about two weeks asking me out, and I finally gave in—we had sex and then eight months later he made me move out of his place so he could move another woman in."

Her story sounds perfectly worthy of a sympathy pint of rocky road ice cream and a hug, doesn't it? Don't you think she got a raw deal? Well, here's what happened when I dug for more details:

Me: How'd he get your e-mail address?
Connie: I posted a personal ad on an Internet board.
Me: What made you place an ad there?
Connie: I'm tired of being alone.
Me: Then what happened?
Connie: Ian answered with a really romantic poem.
Me: What about that intrigued you?
Connie: I like romantic men.
Me: Then what?
Connie: I wrote back to thank him and tell him about myself.
Me: Then what?
Connie: He said he wasn't much for keyboard chat since he only typed five words a minute, so he suggested we talk on the phone.
Me: Was that okay with you?
Connie: Not really. It made him seem like just an ordinary

guy. I wanted more poetry, and I still didn't know much about him. But I gave him my phone number.

Me: So, what made you give him your phone number if you didn't really want to?

Connie: I thought he'd disappear if I didn't, and I was lonely.

Me: What happened next?

Connie: We talked, and to tell you the truth he sounded like a playboy then the way he listed off his conquests and bragged that most of them still wanted him. He hardly asked about me at all. Then he kept calling a couple of times a day for weeks. I guess he wore me down and I thought there might be something more to him, that I was being too snooty.

Me: Then what?

Connie: He invited me to dinner. He was very good looking and complimentary. He forgot his wallet though, so I agreed to pay for dinner. He recited more poetry and kept my wine glass full. When he kissed me good night, he asked what kind of birth control I used.

Me: Did you want to sleep with him?

Connie: Not really, I thought it was quick, and I knew I was sloshed. But after that question, I also figured he was expecting sex, so I went along.

Me: Is that how you felt when you decided to move in with him too?

Connie: Yes.

Me: What were the signs after you moved in with him that he wasn't what you wanted?

Connie: He asked me to pay the rent because he was trying to catch up on his credit card debt, and there were always strange numbers on the caller I.D.

Me: And you stayed because . . . ?

Connie: I didn't want to be alone. Once I've made the mistake of getting "too close" to someone who is not suitable, I'm not real good at breaking up so I tried to make the best of it.

So you see, there were footnotes to Connie's story. She didn't need sympathy ice cream, she needed a mirror. She took out the ad. She gave Ian her phone number. She bedded him. She moved in with him. Are you getting this? Frogs aren't punishment for not saying all of your prayers. They're not the result of some ancient family curse. And they cannot muscle their way into your lives unless you let them. So, do not make the mistake of inviting them in at your weakest points—ordinary cravings, oversights, apathy, and momentary mental lapses—or you'll be telling someone a sorry saga like this one day too.

If you want to date and marry smarter, you're going to have to *pay attention* to what your healthy needs are and whether the man before you is even in the ballpark. And if freaky things happen along the way, run.

What's Stopping You from Having a Prince?

I hope you haven't bought into the popular hype—that I bet was started by a bitter cackle of old maids—that your odds of being hit by a car these days are greater than the odds that you'll stroll down the aisle with Mr. Wonderful. All the good men aren't married, gay, or noncommittal. And they don't really want *Baywatch* babes (that much). If these notions have ever brought on a case of Frog Mind for you, hear ye, hear ye, hear ye: You don't have to dye your hair blond, get a boob job, tan your stretch marks, or move to one of the top ten bachelor capitals of the world. Other than your "blind dates," the two biggest things standing between you and your prince are your negative mating triggers and warped relationship fantasies.

But, before we find out what your normal blackout routines are when it comes to scrutinizing love interests, I want you to write down your story of how you wound up with your last frog. Make sure you include in your essay how you were feeling prior to agreeing to date, live with, or marry him. Write what time of day it was, where you were, what attracted you to him, what your fantasies were about him, and any other factors that made him seemingly irresistible. If you ask yourself, "Then what?" before you move on to a new sentence, you'll get more of the details.

What Is a Negative Mating Trigger?

A negative mating trigger is any small but significant emotion or temptation that can suddenly impair your rational mating sensibilities, making you a prime candidate for Frog Mind. Like kryptonite to Superman, it can render you powerless against your enemies—in this case, frogs. It could be an external trigger: appearance, wallet size, or the amount of baritone in his voice. "I went out with a guy for months even though he still lived with his mom and wore Hooters T-shirts just because he sounded like Barry White."

Internal mating triggers can get you into just as much trouble. Fear, depression, loneliness—they're all breeding grounds for frog binges. Think about it. Are you more likely to latch on to a man who fails the requirements of greatness when you are happy and peaceful, or feeling a little blue, horny or hormonal? When her love life dried up after her divorce, 28-year-old Mattie was terrified of ending up the way her mother did and spending her Friday nights watching old reruns of *The Love Boat* with her cat Fred licking her toes, so she started hanging out at the corner bar. Her last bar beau was—you guessed it—an alcoholic.

Negative triggers leave you at the mercy of your impulses and put you at risk of choosing the wrong men for the wrong reason. If you defuse them, then you can take a more discerning look at a man's frog or prince potential before you invest a lot of time in him.

Here's a list of five common negative mating triggers.

Trigger 1: Physical Attraction

Do you prefer men who are pretty boys with Mr. Universe bodies in Italian suits? Would you find any excuse available to tailgate a man around the mall who looks like he walked out of *GQ* magazine or off the stage of a European fashion show (think Brian McKnight, Brad Pitt, Ricky Martin)? Do you think one of the best things about a new man is how good he will look in a picture with you?

Prospects don't have to be drool-worthy either. If you have a fetish for some outward features like long, thick eyelashes, buff biceps, or tight cheeks you could also be in danger of losing your objectivity too.

For instance, I used to be a sucker for men who spoke with African or Indian accents. When they spoke, fifty percent of my brain synapses shut down. It took three dates with a guy from Ghana for it to dawn on me that he was still hung up on his old girlfriend (and possibly still seeing her) because I was so entranced by the melody of his voice. I also used to get a little woozy over bald guys (if their heads were nicely shaped), dreads and hairy chests.

Rx for cute-guy-itis: Breathe. You're going to have to learn to talk yourself down by asking stabilizing questions like: "Would I be this crazy for him if he got purple leper disease tomorrow?" and "How can I move beyond my shallowness so I can appraise his insides?"

Trigger 2: Negative Emotional States

Do boredom, loneliness, fatigue, depression, fear, stress or desperation drive you to froggy distraction? Do you think of men as surrogate Aladdin lamps: if you rub them enough they'll spit out your heart's desire?

"I'm a loser magnet when I'm depressed," says Mindy, a 27-year-old travel agent, who admits her worst relationships coincide with sad sack bouts of yo-yo dieting. "All the last guy had to do was say he liked big women and I was all over him, hoping his attention would make me feel special and beautiful. But I hit blues bottom one evening when I was eating ice cream in bed, with him lying at my feet. I had to look down over my flabby belly to see him, and I didn't like myself very much at that moment. Nor did I like him for keeping the freezer full of Ben & Jerry's—which he never touched—when he knew I was struggling to be fit and healthy."

Sometimes negative emotions are linked to special places and dates too. Do weddings, clubs, parties and vacations catapult you into a more adventurous anything-goes mood? Do you feel like you need some manly TLC after breakups or around "0" birthdays? Have you ever rolled your eyes at a woman on the beach with hairy armpits because she had a man to lather on her suntan oil and you didn't?

Rx for emotional hara-kiri: If you are ruled by negative emotions, do these two things today. Pinpoint the opposite positive emotion or action and develop an affirmation that you can re-cite to counter the negative emotion. For instance, if boredom triggers irresponsible dating, and you love to bicycle, your affirmation could be, "When I am bored, I bike." Do you see how different this is from "When I am bored, I latch on to the first man I see"?

Trigger 3: Peer Pressure

When comedian Flip Wilson played a sassy, lovable character named Geraldine, if he got caught doing something dubious he'd say, "The devil made me do it." Have you ever blamed your cousin, your neighbor, or the nearest breathing human for your dating mishaps?

"My best friend thinks I should be the beneficiary of her hand-me-down men, but if they were so great, why didn't she keep them?" said 26-year-old Charlotte. "When I worked up the courage to pass one time, she threw such a hissy fit that I gave in and boy, I'd rather eat rotten cabbage than go out with him again. All he talked about was his boooring job. I wanted to say, 'Hello. You're on a date, not the shrink's couch.' And he smacked all through dinner. How can you smack a salad and soup?"

Children can pour on the pressure too. "My ten-year-old started asking for a new daddy in her nightly prayers. Her dad and I divorced two years ago and he dropped out of her life completely. When I knelt next to her I felt like I was this evil, evil witch for depriving her of a father figure, so I've been answering personal ads," said 32-year-old Rosa.

Rx for peer pressure: *Can you say, "None for me, thanks"? If not, practice a hundred times a day until you can.*

Trigger 4: Lust

It is trickier to squash triggers that could give you immediate pleasure. "Sex rules," says 41-year-old Kaitlin. "If I've got the hots for someone and he doesn't entirely gross me out within the first couple of hours, I'm going to sleep with him. Why can't a girl have a sex buddy? And why can't sex lead to a good long-term relationship?"

Lust is a strong emotion that can strike at the least expected moments. "One night, I felt my passion rising and I hit on one of my students' fathers at the Science Night. I started off encouraging him to explore nature with his son who loved birds, and then, much to my surprise (and his), instead of asking 'Do you want me to recommend a bird-watching site,' I asked, 'Do you want me?' " said Angela, a 26-year-old elementary school teacher.

Rx for an overactive libido: A moment of passion can lead to a lifetime memento—a child, a venereal disease. Get a vibrator. Get some batteries. Get some massage oil. And get busy.

Trigger 5: Wallet Size

One night I was sitting in an evening investment class at a local community college and only half listening to the instructor for the first ten minutes, because women kept coming in from the class next door to borrow chairs. There were only ten of us, and apparently dozens of women in the other class. By break time, my curiosity was just killing me, so I tiptoed next door to look at the sign on their door: *How to Marry Rich*. They were on break too, so I tottered in and asked the teacher if the class was typically this full. "Oh, yes," she said, "my classes are always packed. Women want sheiks, men with old money and basketball stars. And there's enough money—I mean men—to go around."

I walked back to my seat next door in a daze, thinking she'd better lighten up on the hair dye because it was destroying her brain cells. The men in my class were all bright single men— two doctors, two lawyers, a couple of 30-something retired Microsoft computer geeks, and several business owners. "What's going on over there?" said one of the doctors who'd seen me on my reconnaissance mission. "They're learning how to marry men with money like you," I said, addressing the whole group. They all scoffed, except for one, who took a suspiciously long bathroom break after my report.

For some women, even prime real estate can deaden their froggy radar. "The thing that made me fall for my current boyfriend was that he had a cottage that was a hundred steps from the beach where he took me every other weekend. His wife made him sell it when she found out about us, and now we have to go to hotels. I miss the waves," said Olga, 26.

Rx for gold-digger-itis: If you grow your own money, then his won't impress you half as much. Three places to start: 401(k), mutual funds, and stocks.

What Are Your Mating Triggers?

By taking a hard look at yourself you can identify the negative triggers that could prevent you from making healthy love choices. Create a chart like this in your R & R Journal and record your temptations for the next ten days.

Date & time	I was at	Feeling kind of	When I saw	I felt like I had to have him because

At the end of ten days, write recovery statements for each trigger.

They should read something like this:

Usually right before I feel an urge to fall for a man, I feel really *(negative emotion),* and I think having him might make me feel more *(opposite positive emotion).*

A better way for me to fill this desire is to *(one of the "Rx" prescriptions).*

Or

I'm attracted to men with _____ because I think I will get _____.

A better way for me to fill this desire is to *(one of the "Rx" prescriptions).*

Read these statements twice a day until you have a healthy handle on your triggers.

Your Fatal Relationship Fantasies

I played Cupid to over 200 singles when I ran a dating service for about a year. One of the first things I asked a client to do was describe their ideal mate and how they would meet. Curiously a lot of the female descriptions sounded like pages out of one of these classic tales:

≈ *Sleeping Beauty.* Here's what 32-year-old Tina had to say: "I think we'll meet on the beach because that's where I think you have to hang out to find guys these days. You've got to let them see the goods. That's what bathing suits are for, right? Then I'll be sunning with my eyes closed and about three layers of suntan oil on, and he will lean down to whisper in my ear, 'Wake up beauty, it's time to go for a swim.' " The other part of this fantasy is that her pre-prince life must remain stale and uninspired. Tina, sadly, has put off buying a house and traveling to Indonesia because she wants to share these milestones with her future husband.

Rx for Sleeping Beauty syndrome: Be an alert beauty and enjoy the life you were given . . . *now.* Sure you can go to the beach to sun, but take a book you love, and make it a beach in Bali if you've always wanted to go.

≈ *Beauty and the Beast* reads a lot like the Frog Prince storyline, but with a bigger, scarier protagonist. "My mom always said you need to give a man a chance, because you never know what kind of life he's had, and that the love of a good woman can turn him around. My ex-husband Jack was a brute who abused me and our son," said 41-year-old Janice, a homemaker. "It took fourteen years to leave him, his marks are still on my body, and somewhere in my heart, I think he might change one day. Isn't that crazy?"

Rx for Beauty and the Beast syndrome: Don't try to fix anything you didn't break. If you want to be charitable, buy books for the church library, volunteer at a senior home, or be a big sister, and then if you still want to cling to redemption theory, wait until the Beast crosses over and has had several years of angelic behavior.

❧ *Cinderella* was a down-on-her-luck type too, but unlike Sleeping Beauty she recruited a wand-waving middle woman, i.e., the fairy godmother. Forty-year-old Kim wants one too. "I told my friends last month that in lieu of a fortieth birthday party, they could find me a man. We'll see what happens." This kind of fantasy can lend itself to bigger fairy godmothers, as described here.

❧ A woman, swept up by the moment, paid $500 to go out on a single date with a singing firefighter at a charity bachelor auction. On my way to the bathroom during one of the breaks, I heard him say to another bachelor, "Man I wonder what she's expecting from me for five hundred dollars. The organizer just said this was a one-time dinner date."

❧ A Minnesota woman won her husband in a mall contest. The groom's friends, determined to find a suitable wife for their buddy, reviewed hundreds of women. The couple met on June 13, 1998, and exchanged vows in Minnesota's Mall of America ninety minutes later.

❧ In 1998 23 million viewers watched Rick Rockwell marry Darva Conger, a total stranger, on a Fox special, *Who Wants to Marry a Millionaire*. She filed to have the marriage annulled days later because of allegations that he had abused a previous girlfriend and just seemed plain creepy. Nevertheless, producers were flooded with thousands of applicants for the next special.

Rx for Cinderella syndrome: Be your own fairy god-mother. Break out your own wand, create your own magic.

Now, what's your favorite relationship fantasy? Is it pro-prince or anti-prince?

Three Ways to Conquer Your Negative Triggers and Relationship Fantasies

Quite simply, negative triggers and relationship fantasies are never going to seem that dangerous in the heat of the moment. You might even recognize them and choose to ignore them any-way, like the lovesick femme fatale I once heard say in a movie "I'd rather have a few moments of passion than a lifetime of noth-ing special." I'm not trying to take your passion. I just want you to save it for a prince. These tips will help you preserve yourself:

1. *Plan ahead.* If you have to attend a friend's wedding in a few months and you know your frog radar might shut down then, start creating a survival strategy. Repeat posi-tive affirmations, use it as an opportunity to practice good behavior, or ask to be part of the planning commit-tee, so you'll have less time to mingle and more time to honor your friend and her new husband.
2. *Be a whistle blower.* Call out your negative triggers and fantasies when they hit. Like the old lumberjacks who used to yell "Timber!" before a tree fell, yelling out your triggers can give your rational mind fair warning that you're in froggy danger. Of course, you'll want to do this in private—in the car, the shower, the backyard, etc.—to avoid calling undue attention to yourself.

3. *Figure out what you really want instead.* If women were really consciously looking for frogs, don't you think there would be more personal ads that read like this? "SBF looking for emotionally abusive, polygamy-minded, partially house-trained wombat who can make my life a living hell." Most women want love, romance, companionship, intimacy and fun. However, when you're stressed to the max, you might reach for a frog when what you really want is *balance, rest, more TLC or more joy.* Learn to tend to your real core needs before you go shopping for a prince.

Recovery Exercises

1. For the next twenty-four hours, every time you get ready to do something unhealthy, say aloud how you are feeling. This will put you in touch with how bad the unhealthy thing sounds before you act, and hopefully change your mind about doing it.
2. Talk to a woman you know is in a healthy relationship and ask her what her relationship fantasies were before she met her beloved, and what they are now.
3. Come up with three ways you can conquer at least one of your negative triggers or relationship fantasies.

R & R Journal exercise: If you haven't already, create the chart on page 48 and record your mating triggers for the next week.

Prince Jeremy

Jeremy, 25, is just a guy with a lot of "nice" genes, says his 23-year-old girlfriend Gail.

Jeremy and I were both enrolled in a personal trainer program at a community college. At first, although his sculpted physique clearly proved that fitness was his calling, I thought he was a total nerd because he carried a briefcase to class instead of a bookbag like the rest of us. He was like the teacher's pet. Always had his homework ready. Always raised his hand to answer the instructor's questions. Always looked excited when we got pop quizzes. Others told him to lighten up, but he'd always say, "I want to be the best." So when he wasn't studying his notes in the student cafe, he scouted for volunteers who would let him practice his newly acquired skills. Some days, I thought he was a show-off. Some days, I admired him.

Halfway through the program I got sick and I was out for a couple of weeks and fell so far behind I almost quit. When Jeremy heard, he offered to help me catch up. It was then I learned that he was working two jobs to help put his baby sister through her last year of college, and rarely slept more than five hours a night. "Sometimes you just have to push through when you know you're doing the right thing no matter how hard it seems," he told me. I stopped whining. Compared to his life, I had it easy. We studied together, we trained together, and I could always talk to him about whatever was on my mind.

As time went by, he did a lot of ordinary things that added up to wonderful. He cut my grass when I was at work, washed my car and clipped my dog's toenails while he quizzed me in preparation for an upcoming test. We became best friends. Eventually he told me he wanted more, but I just didn't feel that "zing," that rush I thought I was supposed to feel, so I kept him at arm's length. And then one day he was bending over to pick up an earring I'd dropped and I caught a good look at his butt, and I thought, "Where have you been, Gail, that you didn't notice this fine feature earlier?" When he returned the earring to my ear, I got the goosebumps I'd been waiting for, and moved in for a kiss.

STEP 3

Pump Yourself Up for the Change

Lesson: Change begins with commitment. Commitment begins with compelling new relationship motivations and a big carrot or a big stick. The activities in this section are designed to help you find yours.

Affirmations

1. It is easy to figure out what motivates me.
2. I always go the distance to get what I want.
3. I'm excited about making positive changes in my love life.

There were once two twin sisters who looked just the same, but acted very differently. One sister, Eve, was happy and upbeat, and whatever she started she finished. She'd run seven marathons, worked her way through college and graduated summa cum laude. Sure, she'd had her share of relationship disasters, but she still believed in love and love believed in her. She stopped dating jerks, she worked on loving herself even more, and soon enough her patience and faith paid off and she met the prince to end all princes. The other sister, Esther, was a sourpuss who always whined about her lot in life—which really was not so bad—and never finished anything she started. If Eve woke her sister to join her in a jog because it was a beautiful day and Esther had told her the night before that she wanted to run, Esther would say, "Not in Alaska," and pull the covers over her head. When her sister dropped out of college in her sophomore year to travel with a rock band, Eve tried in vain to talk her out of it, but Esther, who now bags groceries at the supermarket, told her that college was a waste of time. She also labeled men as a bitter pill, though she often went to bars and went home for one-night stands with guys she was ashamed to be seen with in the light of day. She was jealous of Eve's happy new relationship, jealous of her ability to conquer all with her optimism and hard work. Esther wanted her sister to be more like her, so she asked a wicked witch to cast a spell on her. On the night of her visit, however, the witch couldn't tell the two sisters apart, so she mistakenly cast her spell to make Esther more like Eve. Now, they are both living happily ever after.

Now that you've confessed to your froggy liaisons, forgiven yourself, and found out which fatal triggers and relationship fantasies have thwarted your efforts to find a prince, the biggest challenge ahead is to be more like Eve. Stay optimistic, work hard, and finish what you started. Sure, a life without frogs sounds good right now, doesn't it? But if your enthusiasm and faith wither next week, or next month, or next year, what's going to stop you from morphing back into the Frog Princess? If you are going to permanently position yourself for a prince, you're going to have to generate a guiding force that is bigger than any future froggy lure.

Are You a Wishy Woman?

Remember the woman I told you about back in the Introduction who wanted a bikini body but only came to the club sporadically, half-heartedly pedaled on a stationary bike for a few minutes and then inhaled a hoagie? Well she was a "wishy" woman, who wished she could wear a two-piece, but couldn't motivate herself to pull it off. Can you relate? Have you ever started off with a glint in your eye, a song in your heart, and a gob of good intentions and wound up with the same bad habit again?

Lots of women do. You've heard the old adage "Old habits die hard." Well, frog habits have ninety lives. Breaking them requires vision, compelling motivations, stamina and total buy-in. Otherwise, the moment a strong frog wind blows, you'll be back in the frog pond.

You should know two things up front. One, sometimes when you set out to conquer a bad habit, other parts of you that were comfortable with the old order may start a subconscious resistance movement. When you signed the No More Frogs contract, did *all* of you—the Frog Princess, the Saboteur, Fantasy Girl, the Princess, and whoever else you've got inside of your head who wants to have a say in your love life—cheerily agree to sign it? If you weren't as jazzed up as you would have been to sign your name to a 15-million-dollar sweepstakes claim form, then you've got stragglers. But if you keep sweet-talking them, reminding them of rewards we're going to review in a minute, they'll come around.

Two, the temptations multiply exponentially. For the next few months all your favorite frogs will throw themselves at your feet—big ones, little ones, cute ones, rich ones. It happened to me. I logged more encounters of the froggy kind in those twilight months between Frog Princess and Princess than in my entire mating life. Even after my grandiose rebirthing kick-off ceremony on top of a mountain, which ended with me shouting out to all the plant life below me that I would frog no more, I was still a Wishy Woman for another year, including—I hate to say—several shameless relapses during the first month. The closet smoking naturopath, the moody entrepreneur, the mysterious engineer, and the mute musician. What can I tell you? They came out of nowhere and wooed me mercilessly before I crossed over. Then one day, after many, many affirmations and heart-to-hearts with my inner Frog Princess, I was really healed. At an art exhibit one of the featured artists with thick dreads and an adorable salt-and-pepper beard (both of which I love) flirted with me and then asked me out. Even though I felt aroused just watching his lips form the words, I passed, because I'd watched from a distance as he'd enacted almost the same performance earlier with another woman. That's what I want for you. The courage to say "no" when you know it's not right, and the courage to say "yes" when it is. Do not waste another day, not another moment, with any man who fails your requirements of greatness.

How to Pump Yourself Up for the Change

Eleanor Roosevelt once said that we must do the things we think we cannot. I think the question we fail to ask ourselves when we come up against a challenge is "How did I tackle the last difficult thing in my life?" What resources did you call on to overcome it and how did you make it through the "in-between" time when you were still battling your doubts and resistance? We must also learn to courageously do the things we think we can. Often reviewing past successes can supply you with all the motivation you need to move to the next level in another area of your life. You've had a moment in the sun where you simply felt invincible, haven't you? Recall the most recent one now. Did you lose weight or sculpt your body at the gym? Get a promotion or a great new job? Go on a dream vacation? Buy a house? Pay off all your credit cards? Get your child to stop using the couch as a laundry bag for play clothes? What was it for you? And more important, what motivated you to do it? See if one of the items below rings true for you:

I wanted more . . .	I wanted less . . .
Pleasure	Pain
Pride	Shame
Joy	Sadness
Courage	Fear
Love	Hate
Strength	Weakness
Peace	Chaos

Now, think about two other times you moved a mountain. Which of the factors above motivated you to succeed then?

If most of your picks were from the first column, you'll be able to keep yourself motivated to adopt healthier partnering strategies by focusing on the carrots, or positive rewards, that lie ahead. If you leaned toward column two, then you may respond better to sticks, negative consequences of not following through.

If Carrots Motivate You

Decide today that there is a big, juicy treat on the other side of your frog purge. Maybe a prince, or maybe something with its own personal glory like bliss or self-mastery. Make it the kind of desire that Oprah Winfrey once said "is so bright it almost burns your eyes."

Many years before my honey and I discovered each other, I declared to my other single friends that I was creating a wonderful life for myself, and would have a prince in no time. Two of these friends often invited themselves over to hear my fireside stories, and they sat around me like children listening to stories of Santa's arrival on Christmas Eve. *They believed because I believed.* One of the sweetest truths I know is that you will always get what you want if the desire is strong enough and you hang in there forever until you get it.

Hazel, 25, finally gave up lying, cheating playboy types after a week-long meditation retreat. "I felt so incredibly calm and centered for the first time in years, and I knew I wanted to create a more peaceful life."

Jewel, 33, a former mistress to an investment tycoon, reached her turning point the night her 10-year-old twin daughters announced over dinner that they wanted to marry someone rich or famous like one of the Backstreet Boys, because then they'd be somebody in the world. "I wanted to teach them to love themselves more, but how could I teach what I didn't yet know?" She wrote this recovery pledge note to herself that night, broke up with Daddy Warbucks and read it every day for a year:

Dear Jewel,

You are a precious treasure. Today and always, I love who you are and who you are coming to be. You're funny, smart, and kind, and you make me proud. I expect you to forever be something better than you were yesterday, and to choose a man who's yours, all yours, who simply cherishes you. The girls are watching and so am I.

Your BIGGEST fan

Recovering joy can be a big carrot motivation too. "No one knows this about me," says 28-year-old Anna, "but before my last two bad relationships I used to sing around the house every day, and it made me happy inside." After living with her last mentally abusive boyfriend for four years, she packed her bags while he was at work, singing one of her favorite songs all the while, something she hadn't done since she'd moved in with him. "I was kind of scared about how I'd make it without him—terrified, really—but the familiar joy and comfort in my song gave me the strength I needed to leave."

Sometimes a glimpse at another woman's prince can inspire. These three women were vicariously persuaded to seek healthier partners:

- ❧ "I just get the feeling that my sister's husband will always adore her no matter what. Last weekend I went to visit them, and she was just getting over a cold. She didn't have a lick of makeup on and she was wearing a really tacky old dress, but he kept his arm around her on the couch, nuzzling her neck the whole time anyway."

- ❧ "When my best friend left her job as an attorney to be a full-time stay-at-home mom, she and her husband had to move to a smaller home and sell his boat, but her husband never once complained. My ex-boyfriend even tried to rile him by saying, "You should be more of a man and make her get her butt back to work and put the kids in daycare where they belong so you can keep your boat." And you know what he said? "Sure, I'll miss the money and my boy toys, but look what she gave up, a successful ten-year law practice. She's made a smart choice for our family, and I'm proud of her."

- ❧ "My son's drama teacher's husband always runs up on the stage after the last cast curtsy and hands his wife a bouquet of roses. You'd think her play was debuting on Broadway or something instead of a middle school auditorium. It's so sweet."

Now, it's your turn. Get your R & R Journal and write down ten positive rewards that you might get out of adopting healthier mating habits, and when you're done put the three most exciting ones on index cards in the following format:

I'm motivated to release my old Frog Princess self because I want more _____ in my life. When I cross over, I'll feel more _____ and look _____.

Recite these phrases as often as you can throughout the day. If you think it would fire you up more to make a song out of them, do it.

The other sweet rewards of good behavior. Yeah, yeah, yeah. Keeping yourself motivated to stay away from frogs has its own intrinsic reward, but why can't a new dress say "atta girl" too? Complete the worksheet below and treat yourself to a dress, a CD, a pair of earrings, or some pleasurable victory token when you reach these milestones, because you've earned it, baby.

The Rewards of Being a Good Girl

First 3 days:
When I have honored my No More Frogs Pledge for 3 days I will treat myself to _____.

First week:
When I have honored my No More Frogs Pledge for 7 days I will treat myself to _____.

Second week:
When I have honored my No More Frogs Pledge for 14 days I will treat myself to _____.

First month:
When I have honored my No More Frogs Pledge for one month I will treat myself to _____.

3 months:
When I have honored my No More Frogs Pledge for 3 months I will treat myself to _____.

6 months:
When I have honored my No More Frogs Pledge for 6 months I will treat myself to a weekend getaway or _____.

Rack up these bonuses for staving off old negative triggers:
Whenever I resist giving in to my _____ trigger, I will reward myself with _____.
Whenever I resist giving in to my _____ trigger, I will reward myself with _____.
Whenever I resist giving in to my _____ trigger, I will reward myself with _____.

Note: None of your rewards should involve seeing, touching or otherwise fiddling with a frog.

If Sticks Motivate You

If you're a stick-motivated person, then you're going to have to come up with a scary stick. The more it makes you quake in your pumps, the better. Think big-time pain, shame, sadness or fear. Think about your worst frog souvenir. Think about one of the scenes that came up back in the Scared Straight exercise in Step 1. Think about anything that makes the idea of being with another frog as tempting as eating a handful of crunchy, live beetles.

Here are the repulsive stick catalysts that carried four women through their frog recoveries:

- ❧ *Pain:* "When I found out my husband was cheating on me with my best friend behind my back for two years, I felt like someone had lanced my heart. I went through two months of hell, barely eating or sleeping, and when I walked there was this awful, awful pain in my bones that wouldn't go away."
- ❧ *Shame:* "A new guy who answered my personal ad told me he hated children and I pretended for three months of dating that I didn't have a son."
- ❧ *Sadness:* "My ex-fiancé called our wedding off four times in the three years we were engaged. Each time after months of crying, suffering and Prozac, he knocked on my door, said he was sorry and that he loved me. I *never* want to go there again."
- ❧ *Fear:* "My ex-husband spanked our then four-year-old daughter for spilling milk on the carpet so hard he broke her leg. After years of abuse, I decided that day that I had to protect both of us."

Got your stick yet? If not, here are some other precious things you could lose if you don't cut frogs loose:

Family ties. One woman's family disowned her completely when she moved to another city to shack up with her Internet boyfriend of a year. And believe it or not, a few months after she arrived, he went back to his old girlfriend, leaving her homesick and alone in a new city with a job that barely covered the rent. Another woman's father took her out of his will when she married an alcoholic. When she begged him to reconsider, he said flatly, "I've worked hard to leave a rich legacy to my family. Do you want me rolling around in my grave wondering if your boozing husband is drinking up your inheritance?"

Parental interference launched another woman's frog recovery too. Her mom withheld her blessing (and her wedding dress) until 29-year-old Tia used her pre-wedding gift—ten paid visits to a shrink. "As it turns out, after a few sessions, which I needed more than I knew, I realized my mom wasn't the only one who thought my future husband was creepy. Deep down, I did too, so I called the wedding off."

Your assets. Forget about being cut out of your parents' will, and not getting to wear your mother's wedding dress if she rejects your beloved. Does the phrase "being taken to the cleaners" ring any bells for you? One woman I talked to actually dipped into her son's college fund at her underemployed boyfriend's request to purchase a brand-new designer wardrobe for him. Other sugar mamas co-signed loans, made His and Her car payments, and doled out generous cash gifts. Mercy.

A few were even taken to the *big cleaners*, like the real estate agent who made about $300,000 a year who was ordered to pay $3,000 a month in temporary maintenance to her Nintendo-playing ex-husband since she was the sole breadwinner.

Your career. Frogs can jeopardize your career advancement potential too, which takes its toll on your take-home. Thirty-three-year-old Malia lost a promotion she'd been working on for years when her ex got drunk at a Christmas party and tried to tongue-kiss her boss under the mistletoe. "I think the only reason my boss kept me on after that was because I'd already built strong relationships with our clients, but no big raise and no new title." What about the little ways frogs can whittle away at your work productivity? Some women blame them for increased sick and tardy days and personal calls at work, and being the subject of office gossip.

Your reputation. Avoiding public embarrassment can be a great motivator. "My elderly neighbor once overheard my ex-fiancé call me a stupid whore in the driveway. I felt her out the next day—since I knew she was the block gossip—by apologizing for the disturbance and claiming that he had Tourette's syndrome and couldn't help himself. Nevertheless, for about a month all her little old lady friends in the neighborhood were suspiciously unresponsive when I waved to them on my evening jogs," said 29-year-old Joanie.

Your dignity. During my research interviews, infidelity was the most commonly cited reason for losing face in a relationship. Popular infidelity scenarios included boyfriends and husbands sleeping with a best friend or relative, co-worker, old girlfriend and women of the night. The kicker? Nine times out of ten the women were more furious with the other woman than they were their frog. A woman who was married for fourteen years said, "My ex-husband had a side affair with my shady cousin for ten years of our marriage. She even slept with him the morning of our wedding. I knew she was sort of slimy, but I never expected her to stoop so low." Another woman surprised her husband with a picnic dinner at his office (because he'd been putting in late hours for weeks) and found him on his office couch stroking his naked partner, Dennis. "That Dennis is a snake," she hissed.

On a more reassuring note, only a few of the women who ever had to sit through an Al-Anon meeting or track down their jewelry or silver at a pawn shop needed supplemental stick motivations to permanently ditch men with alcohol and drug habits.

Now, write down ten negative consequences of not adopting healthier mating habits, and when you're done put the three most frightening ones on index cards in the following format:

I'm motivated to release my old Frog Princess self because I want less _____ in my life. When I cross over, I'll experience less _____ and more _____.

Installing Your Motivating Statements

I worked with 27-year-old Jamie on her frog recovery motivational statements, and we came up with three that she was very charged about. However, a few days later she called me up and said they weren't working and she was thinking about going clubbing.

"How often are you saying them?" I asked. And after a long pause she said, "Oh, I thought after you made me say them a zillion times the other day (she was exaggerating, mind you), that was enough."

"You have to keep saying them aloud with conviction, every day, as often as you need to, until they take—until you lose your desire for clubbing," I told her.

And then in my mind's eye I could see her nodding her head, but then she presented resistance thought number 1. "I can't do that. My roommate is going to think I'm nuts."

"So? Do you want to change or not?" I said.

"Every day?" she said.

"Every day."

And then I told her what I'm going to tell you now. As a complement to my frog recovery, I was celibate for three years so I could tend to personal growth and mothering, and frankly, because I wanted to retrain myself to view sex as more of a sacred act that I shared with my next someone special. I couldn't have pulled either objective off with wimpy motivations. Yes, I dated the last year, but I never had sex with my dates. Not even with A or R—whom I would like to personally nominate for award-winning begging-for-sex lines.

How'd I do it? Every morning for about three months, I got up, went to the mirror and recited one of my motivational statements as many times as I could before it was time to get dressed and take Esprit to school and myself to work. And then I let the vibrations echo throughout my mind for the rest of the day. That's my prescription for you too. If you want to make an honest Princess out of yourself, you have to build the momentum and keep it going. You've got to burn the new, healthy incentives you've just discovered into your soul. You will have to know them by heart. You will have to start dreaming about them.

Other Pumper-uppers

Attitude and variety will also help keep your motivation high and lay the foundation for change work ahead.

1. *Feel blessed, not burdened.* My honey, Imhotep, has been a vegan for about twenty years, which means he doesn't eat animal products or by-products. Not surprisingly a lot of people tend to initially presume he's a tor-

tured soul who has to pray down daily hankerings to spin through the drive-in at Burger King or Pizza Hut for some "normal" food instead of his gourmet plant meals. But if pressed, he says "I don't consider this a burden. I love what I eat and what it does for my body." This is the attitude that will help you remain motivated to find your prince.

2. *Motivate yourself with music.* Adopt a motivating theme song like the tune from *Rocky*, or try one of the songs from the Olympics, like "Give Me One Moment in Time." "I Believe I Can Fly" by R. Kelly is also one of my personal pump-me-up favorites. Play your theme song a few times in the morning and then again at bedtime before reading your motivating statements.

3. *Ask yourself these Daily Power questions:* (1) What do I want? (2) What is important about having it? (3) What will I get out of it? (4) How will I feel when I have it? (5) How will it change my life? (6) What will it take for me to get it and is it worth it? (7) What step can I take, at this moment, to have what I want?

4. *Model yourself after women you know who have princes or are frog-free.* Find out what their relationship motivations are, watch the way they carry themselves and how they behave in the world, and make like a copycat.

5. *Choose a cheerleader.* This would be your best girlfriend or a supportive relative who wants to see you win at healthy love. Pick someone you'd nominate for lifetime cheerleader award, tell her about your new relationship goals, and ask her to pitch you a few perky calls a day or give you a weekly motivational check-up for your first month.

Handling Motivational Slumps

If you're like most people, you're not going to be up twenty-four-seven. Sorry. For that matter, you might have whole days when you don't have an ounce of enthusiasm for your pledge, not one single rah-rah-rah. You might even hang up on your get-happy cheerleader when she calls. But try not to let these moments zap your long-term commitment. *Hold on.* They are just part of the conflicting feelings you occasionally have to wade through until good habits become second nature. Here are two of the best ways I know to beat motivational blahs.

1. *Push through.* When it comes to motivation, 100 percent authenticity 100 percent of the time can be overrated. I believe in the "Do" motivational model. If you do it, you'll get it done. Why can't you fake it until you feel it? Do you think Tina Turner is bubbling over with enthusiasm before each of her concerts? I bet sometimes her feet hurt, or she's got period cramps, or is in a tizzy over her hair or makeup. And yet, she manages to put all that aside and strut up to the stage and deliver the kind of dazzling performances that always let you know why she's been one of America's favorite pop queens for decades. I promise you if you're in any kind of slump, if you force yourself to get up and briskly walk around the neighborhood (or your apartment), your attitude will also change, and you'll feel more like doing what you need to do to create change in your life.

2. *Hang out.* Rest breaks are good also. If you've been pushing through and pushing through and pushing through, you might need a respite. Once I watched a glassblower making a beautiful glass vase. She put the fire to a piece of raw glass. Then she let it cool. Then she put the fire to

it again, and let it cool. Over and over again she did this, and eventually, she had a stunning vase. If you've properly installed your initial motivations, give them time to cool, and then if you don't see your dream taking shape, put the fire to it again.

Your Motivational Speech

Some day, you're going to mentor another woman or a young girl who wants to make positive changes in her mating habits. Did you know that? We learn, then we do, and then we teach. What will you tell her when she asks you how you kept the faith? How you stayed motivated? In a few minutes, I want you to find a comfortable chair and close your eyes and count backwards from 25 to 1, relaxing each part of your body from head to toe. When you reach the number 1, imagine you are on a podium in front of an auditorium full of women and young girls. They are honoring you today as a Woman of Achievement, and want you to tell them how you managed to turn your love life around. Picture yourself telling them your inspiring recovery story and closing with a standing ovation.

Recovery Exercises

1. Watch a motivational movie like *Mulan*.
2. Buy (or make) five small items that symbolize the new you and the healthier relationship commitment you've made and put them in a keepsake box. For example, your box might contain a picture of a happy couple, a heart-shaped pendant, small slips of paper with the words

"peace," "power," "courage," "joy" and "wisdom" written on them, a silk rose, and a miniature copy of the book *The Little Engine That Could*. Open your box every day and review its contents.

R & R Journal exercise: Write about another time you kept yourself motivated and how that experience will help keep you motivated to stay frog-free.

Prince Brian

Brian, 36, is a program manager for a large software company. He has been married for nine years to his 36-year-old wife, Alma, a retired software test engineer and business owner.

At their tenth wedding anniversary party last year at one of their favorite restaurants with about fifty members of their family and friends looking on, Alma's mother gave a toast. "You always hope when your children are little that when they grow up and go into the world, they will find kind, honest, decent people to love. And I guess we've known since the start with Brian that our prayers had come true."

As I sat there watching them gaze lovingly into each other's eyes, I remembered how Alma told me a long time ago that she first fell in love with Brian because he was her best friend and the smartest man she knew, but she *grew* to love him more because he had this endearing, enduring quality about him that has seen them both through tough financial and health hardships. "We barely had two nickels to rub together when we first got married, and then I became quite ill and told him that he should divorce me. He looked at me and said, 'I waited too long for you to give you up now. I knew in ninth-grade Spanish class that I would marry you, and I'm not going anywhere.' "

Amazingly, Brian balances a demanding full-time job, parenting their 4-year-old daughter Kamilah, and helping Alma manage her health challenges, while still making her feel like the queen of the castle. "He never complains. Not even when I'm crabby because I'm sick. He just does what has to be done, whether it's fixing dinner or taking Kamilah to work with him, or nuzzling my neck when I'm having a bad health day." Brian has also had to artfully negotiate with his entrepreneurial wife to rest and delegate some of her business affairs. "A few weeks ago I told him I needed to take a business trip to South Africa and I knew he was going to explode. And he did. He was rightfully worried and scared, and joined my doctor in a protest. But in the end, he helped me pack, made me promise to come home immediately at whatever cost if I needed medical attention and took me to the airport and kissed me goodbye. I will always love him for that."

STEP 4

Live Juicy

Lesson: If you cultivate an enchanting, captivating love affair with yourself, filled with savory pleasures and juicy delights, there won't be any room in your life for frogs.

Affirmations

1. I take time to cherish myself and to grow a life that I love.
2. I was born for glory.
3. I live juicy.

Becca had spent many days and nights thinking about her dubious dating sagas, and she wanted to change things. No frog would ever dupe her into a kiss again. But now that she was on the wagon, there was a void, not unlike the emptiness she felt when she had to give her pet collie away after he bit the neighbor kid. The days weren't so bad. There was work. But the nights sucked. How would she survive them without at least a dozen more cable channels? Glumly, she wandered out to her mailbox to retrieve the day's offerings, and there in her mailbox sat a lone brochure for a new dance center. "Can you tango?" it read. "No," she thought, beginning to smile, "not yet."

Are you living a life you love? Or are you muddling through, living what an observant poet once called a life of quiet desperation? Do you know what a gift your life is, and how to enjoy each second of unwrapping it? Do you know that it's possible to go from joy to joy to joy by being your truest self, stepping up the TLC, following a dream, and honoring your spirit?

Learn to Love Your Life (Even Without a Man)

One night my daughter, Esprit, was having a conversation with one of her friends about another classmate who was going to a dance stag. It went something like this:

Esprit: Did you know so-and-so was going to the dance alone?

Friend: Didn't any boys ask her?

Esprit: Yeah, a coupla guys—even one of the football players.

Friend: Well, what happened?

Esprit: She turned them all down.

Friend (on the verge of hyperventilating): She what?

Esprit: She said, "Girl Power! I'm going alone." I heard her. Then she even said she was going to get a new dress and purse because she was worth it. Wasn't that a line in a hair commercial?

Friend: Oh my God, are you for real?

They thought their friend was a freak of nature. I thought she was divine. I also heard a grown woman call a radio talk show for advice on getting over her ex-boyfriend. The host told her to get dressed to the nines and make herself a dinner reservation for one at her favorite restaurant. "That's crazy," she replied. "What would make me get all dressed up for myself?"

What would make *you* slip into an outfit you adore and take yourself out on the town? If you are going to live juicy, make the answer to that question a daily practice. The following exercises will guide you through a process of self-discovery in which you'll discover how to infuse more passion and joy into your life—how to live juicy.

Four Surefire Ways to Live Juicy

One: Be at Home with Yourself

When you were a child, you were probably very at home with yourself. You may have scribbled on your toes with magic markers and streaked your hair with them too. If you had a milk mustache at the dinner table, you didn't care because you were too busy arranging your peas in the shape of a smiley face in the mashed potatoes. You said "no" when you didn't want to do something, and you meant it. You were simply *you*. And then one day, you noticed that your toes weren't exactly the same size; that your hair was either too straight or too curly, and someone chastised you for not doing *what they wanted you to do*. Little by little, the "real" you went into deep disguise to avoid disapproval, ridicule and rejection, and in time, you forgot how good it felt just being you. I suspect that there is still a quiet part of you that remembers, that probably surfaces when you are alone, or with your best friend. What would you say if I told you that giving her a coming out party could quickly put the juicy back into your life? If you don't have time to really be you, who do you have time to be?

How to Be at Home with Yourself Again

1. Redecorate one room of your house with colors, textures, photos and furniture until it represents your truest self.
2. In the next thirty days, do three things that you've put off because of what other people might think, but that you really want to do. (Turn the volume up in the car when you hear a song you like, and start bopping your head and snapping your fingers. If you want a red BMW with a sunroof and you can afford it, buy it. If you want to have your navel pierced so you can wear a diamond stud in it, do it.)
3. Replace three items that don't express your authentic self and never will, with items that do. You will know these items of clothing, music, jewelry, knickknacks, etc., by the fact that you've dearly neglected them or cringed at the thought of having to go near them for a very long time. Perhaps you originally bought them under familial, advertising or trend pressure, but they just were never quite you. Thirty-nine-year-old Deidra, for example, accepted her grandmother's expensive birthday and Christmas gifts of classic jewelry and stuffed them into her bureau, but felt most at home in the bohemian-looking beaded chokers and silver earcuffs she bought at craft fairs.
4. Spend at least five minutes each day appreciating your morning face before you put your makeup on. Wash it slowly and lovingly, and then trace each part of it in the mirror with your eyes.
5. Say "no" to the next ten people who ask you to do something you don't really want to do (yes, even if you've done it a hundred times before). And then when you're alone again, shout out "Yes!"

Two: Build a Dream

Martha Graham once said, "There is only one of you in all time, this expression is unique, and if you block it, it will never exist through any other medium; and [it will] be lost." What are you here to do? Raise a healthy garden or a healthy child? Write a book that will change someone's life or improve the human condition? Design a new clothing line or an orphan's Halloween costume? Lobby for a legislative initiative or register people to vote? Building a dream can help you leave an unmistakable testament to your own unique expression, and keep you energized and purposeful every single day of your life.

Take a look at how these women built (or are building) their dreams:

- ❧ "I got my pilot's license last year," said one divorcée. "When I was five or six, I went around the house with both arms outstretched like I was a bird in flight. I *really* wanted to fly, but I put that dream on hold for two decades and got married and raised two children instead. Now, I *fly* down to see them every other weekend." —*Sylvia, 46*
- ❧ "When I was fifteen, I decided I wanted to be a millionaire, so I put money from baby-sitting, birthdays and holidays into a savings account. My mom put my money into a mutual fund two years later, and now that I'm out of college in my first professional job, I funnel half of my salary into investments. My net worth is sixty thousand dollars." —*Paloma, 23*
- ❧ "I started a non-profit organization called H.O.M.E. to educate women about home ownership, credit, banking and budgeting." —*Angela, 33*

How you can build your dream(s)

1. Find something that's important to you, that embraces your values, passions or hobbies, and develop a dream builder statement. Ideas: (1) Do something to better the world; (2) Do something to better your neighborhood; (3) Do something to better your family; (4) Support a friend's dream; (5) Do something to help people who cannot care for themselves; (6) Champion a cause you feel strongly about.
   Examples of Dream Builder statements: (1) I will spearhead fundraisers for a new playground for the elementary school; (2) I will open a boutique with my sister; (3) I will write books that spread joy, inspiration and empowerment to women; (4) I will join the prayer circle at church.
2. Start a list of fun things you'd like to do in your lifetime. *Examples:* (1) I will sail down the Nile; (2) I will own a Porsche; (3) I will live on an island; (4) I will collect unusual teddy bears.
3. Focus on a particular area of your life and then come up with a monthly mini-mission for each thing (career, health, financial, social, spiritual).
4. Scan the newspapers for inspiring human-interest stories, and then write one of those people to see how they got started, or if they need your help.

Three: Ignite Your Pampering Flame

When most of the world was stockpiling canned and dry goods, batteries and flashlights for the Y2K scare, I was hoarding body butter, bath salts, facial masks, aromatherapy candles and herbal teas. TLC has often been the link between an ordinary moment and a juicy one and it makes me feel good. If you follow these steps, you can become a pampered princess too.

⇨ ***Step 1: Know what makes you feel pampered.*** Biking through the park on a sunny day makes some women sigh. For others it's flowers, silk sheets or Saturday morning cartoons. Create a Master Pampering list of at least ten things that utterly delight you, and keep it handy.

⇨ ***Step 2: Budget it in.*** Setting aside a regular stash for your TLC supplies means you'll never have to fork over your massage money for the light bill. If money is tight, think low-budget decadence. Instead of a $60 massage, splurge on a box of Calgon, a bunch of flowers and two candles ($10) or buy a fresh papaya ($2) and rub it on your face for a few minutes for an exfoliating aromatherapy treatment.

The Pampered Princess's Shopping List

For	*Stock up on*
Hands	❑ Nail polish and nail glitter ❑ Cuticle soak ❑ Scented moisturizers ❑ Colorful nail files ❑ Rings
Face	❑ Facial masks ❑ Lipstick or scented lip balm ❑ Fruity toners ❑ Eye pillows ❑ Earrings ❑ Silky moisturizers ❑ Tweezers ❑ Face glitter

For	Stock up on
Legs and Feet	❑ Paraffin ❑ Toe separators ❑ Odd-shaped pumice stones ❑ Toenail clippers ❑ Nail polish ❑ Foot cream and powder ❑ Colorful razors ❑ Warm, cushy socks or slippers
Hair	❑ Aromatic shampoos and conditioners ❑ Hair jewelry ❑ Hot oil treatments ❑ Pretty scarves
Whole body	❑ Bath pillows ❑ Herbal soap ❑ Body butter ❑ Bath salts, bubble bath and bath gels ❑ Bath seltzers ❑ Body wrap treatments ❑ Body brush or loofah sponge ❑ Temporary henna tattoos ❑ Lingerie

❧ *Step 3: Pencil it in.* Give yourself two opportunities each day to indulge in something on your Master Pampering list. If you have a cat, she could be the purrfect pampering alarm clock. Follow her lead when you see her settling down for TLC.

❧ *Step 4: Savor it.* This is probably a given, but you should not be lounging in front of your fireplace in your favorite robe paying your bills, or worrying about the report due at work, or on the phone gossiping with your girlfriend. You should, however, be laid back on a dozen pillows, listening to music you love, letting the flames relax and nourish you. As you do this day after day after day, you'll build up your comfort reserve.

Cleopatra Who? What Some Women Have Done in the Name of Pampering

- "I have a spa day in my home on the last day of the month. The night before I prepare a special wild greens salad with walnuts and raspberry vinaigrette for lunch. In the morning I make a couple of scones, a large pot of Pineapple-Mint tea and a pitcher of lemon water to sip on. Then I line up head-to-toe pampering goodies and magazines, and oh boy." —*Leah*, 33
- "In the summer, I wrap myself in a silk sheet and settle down in my porch swing with a cup of tea to watch the sunrise. It is sheer heaven." —*Mona*, 41
- "As a young girl, I loved grab bags, so I label plain paper bags 'Face,' 'Hands,' 'Feet' and 'Hair' and fill them with travel-size pampering products. It's always a surprise to open one and spoil that lucky part of my body. Sometimes I prepare them for pregnant girlfriends, too, as a reminder not to skimp on the TLC." —*Colleen*, 24

Four: Spend Quality Time with Yourself

Pampering is one way to spend quality time on your body, but don't take your spirit for granted either. Replenish it with at least thirty to sixty minutes of alone time each day, doing little more than listening to the sound of your own heartbeat. Here's how:

- Have morning and evening quiet time in meditation, prayer or gratitude thoughts.

❧ Create a Not-to-Do List one weekend a month, and do everything on it. (i.e., *1. Do not* run any errands this weekend; *2. Do not* do any major household chores; *3. Do not* get out of bed in a rush or one second before I absolutely want to; *4. Do not* answer the phone all weekend; *5. Do not* worry about my troubles or anyone else's.)

❧ Have a monthly day of silence. Turn off the phone, the TV, and the radio, and do everything in slow motion, observing your thoughts and the landscape around you. This will sharpen your hearing, eyesight, taste, and touch and teach you how to revel in the peace of your own essence.

❧ Take yourself away from your "normal" life for a weekend, a week, or longer if you have unused vacation time. On her 45th birthday, one corporate executive took a five-week "walkabout," which is an old aboriginal tradition of taking a break from work to go on a long, solitary, contemplative walk in the bush. For you, "the bush" could be a walking trail near your home, driving down to the beach or up to a mountain retreat, or slipping off on a virtual mental vacation to think about your life in a slightly different way.

Will You Scare Men Off If You Can Make the Earth Move for Yourself?

Yes, and no. When you start to live juicy, most frogs will either run for the pond or try to sabotage you. Why? They know the more you increase your self-pleasuring prowess the less you'll be beholden to them for care or comfort. But when a prince—

and that's what you want—catches you pampering yourself or spinning a dream, he will, as my honey says, stand taller and love you even more because your joy becomes his joy.

I'll never forget the time an event planner I thought I was interested in stood me up. After waiting on him for fifteen minutes, I suspected that he was smoothing out a sudden snag in his upcoming event. After fifteen more minutes, I wondered if I'd missed a daylight savings shuffle. After another fifteen minutes, I imagined he'd contracted laryngitis, and was too weak to even pick up the phone and breathe hard into it so that I'd know he'd at least made the courteous effort. After fifteen more minutes, I headed for the restaurant where we'd made reservations and had an absolutely wonderful dinner. The next day, I called him (note, *I* called *him*), and explained that unlike the average woman, when a man stands me up I assume he's at death's door. He said he was sorry (now that I had him on the phone), but he was feeling a little insecure about our date. "You buy yourself flowers. You cook yourself fancy Thai dishes. You make your own candles. You always look stunning even if you're just going to the grocery store. You own a drill. What can I offer you?"

My truth: If he didn't know, I didn't want him. If your self-care protocol intimidates any man then he's not the one for you. Hold out for a prince who knows that two who enjoy themselves, can enjoy each other all the more.

Your Right to Live Juicy

My co-worker Marci, mother of two, had been trying to muster up the gumption to enroll in massage school and up her TLC quotient, so one day I bought her a pampering basket and a bottle of sparkling cider and told her I wanted to toast her new life. And that's when she started to backpedal.

Marci: I'd almost rather empty garbage cans than work here anymore, but I think I can hang out until the kids are off to college. It's only four more years.

Me: What's stopping you from signing up for massage school today?

Marci: I'd be neglecting the kids, wouldn't I? It's bad enough their dad doesn't give them the time of day since the divorce, but they need me.

Me: How much of your time would they lose if you went back to school?

Marci: About six hours a week of class time, and then I'll have to put in three more hours a week for clinic practice after a few months. Who's going to cook on the nights when I'm in class?

Me: What would they gain?

Marci (her eyes lighting up): I'd be happier. I love massage and I want to build my life around it.

It was hard work juggling the demands of her day job, school, and motherhood, but Marci is now a practicing massage therapist. In her office hangs a poster her daughters gave her that reads: YOU DID IT, MOM! WE'RE SO PROUD!

If you have any pangs of guilt about your right to live juicy, and feel like you need permission from anyone else to get started today, I now bestow upon you the following rights:

1. As long as you are not being a public nuisance or doing something illegal or immoral, you have the right to be yourself in private and in public.

2. You have the right to build big dreams and little dreams, and to celebrate each and every one of them.
3. You have the right to pamper yourself; to buy as many bottles of bubble bath as you want and can afford.
4. You have the right to wear the clothes you love, whenever you want.
5. You have the right to spend time each day meditating or being still.
6. You have the right to use your sick days at work to nurture yourself. (It's called preventative pampering.)
7. You have the right to nod at anyone who disagrees with your right to be you, or to care for yourself, as though they have mental problems.
8. You have the right to expect your children to survive without you while you take time to take care of yourself, or to hire a baby-sitter to watch them while you do.
9. You have the right to post DO NOT DISTURB signs in your home sanctuary, turn off the phone and otherwise ignore the demands of the outside world.
10. You have the right not to wait until your birthday, a major holiday, or the day after a nervous breakdown to do any of these things.

Recovery Exercises

1. Make a collage of things you enjoy or are hoping to enjoy.
2. Fill your calendar for the upcoming week with pampering appointments.
3. Think of something you really want to do, but have been putting off, and take one step toward it today.

R & R Journal exercise: Add ten more things to your list of things you'd like to do in your lifetime.

Prince Kurt

Kurt Warner is a quarterback for the St. Louis Rams. And, as I learned in a feature article about him in USA Today, *he is also Brenda Warner's husband and Zachary, Jesse and Kade's doting father.*

Brenda's romance with Kurt began long before he became the NFL's most valuable player after five months as a Rams pro quarterback. She was 24, he was 20, and they met while taking line-dancing lessons at a Cedar Falls, Iowa, country music bar. At the end of their first barn dance, Brenda told him she had two children—Zachary and Jesse—and that Zachary, then 7, had special needs because his father, Brenda's first husband, had accidentally dropped him during a bath as an infant.

She thought that was the last she'd see of Kurt. But the next morning, he showed up to meet Zachary and his sister, Jesse, with a rose in his hand. "He fell in love with the kids before he fell in love with me," Brenda says.

After their wedding, Kurt adopted both Zachary and Jesse, and they moved in with Brenda's parents. By day, he trained. By night, he stocked shelves at a grocery store in Iowa for $5.50 an hour. Nowadays, other clerks are stocking the shelves with Kurt's cereal, Warner's Krunch Time. Kurt has also been on the cover of *Sports Illustrated* and featured in *People Magazine*, and yet one of his favorite keepsakes is a gigantic card his children (including the newest addition to the family, baby Kade) surprised him with made out of Rams blue and gold paper. Written in childlike doodles and surrounded by hearts are the words, "You're as Great a Dad as you are a Quarterback."

If Kurt were going to make a card for Brenda, it might say, "You're as great a mom as you are my hero." After Zachary's accident she'd received a hardship discharge from the Marines.

When she was eight months pregnant with Jesse, she filed for divorce from her first husband, moved in with her parents and signed up for food stamps. Her parents were killed in 1996 after a tornado demolished their retirement home. "She has shown me the best way to respond when you go through struggles—by resisting self-pity and handling her life with poise and grace. She's a tremendous inspiration to me," says Kurt, who routinely shares a post-game kiss with his wife.

STEP 5

Throw All the Frogs
Back in the Pond

Lesson: If you were starting a new diet, wouldn't you chuck the Belgian chocolate, the chocolate raspberry cheesecake, and the Hershey's chocolate syrup? Well, if you are going to reshape your love life, then Brute, Boy-Boy, Icy and the gang will have to go too.

Affirmations

1. I now have the courage to give frogs the boot.
2. Whenever I release an unhealthy relationship I grow more powerful and peaceful.
3. I enjoy relinquishing reminders that keep unhealthy connections alive.

Many years ago, I read a story about a girl summoning a genie and asking for a chest of diamonds and a castle by the sea. The genie told her she'd have to eat three live frogs before he'd do her bidding. She, of course, shivered at the thought and told him she'd have to think about it. Off she went to consult a mountain sage for advice. "How can I eat three icky frogs?" she asked him. He smiled and told her to eat the biggest one first while thinking of the diamonds and the castle, and the second and third would seem easy. And that's exactly what she did. She lined all the frogs up, and swallowed them one by one, with an image of herself sitting in her castle, wearing a diamond tiara, sipping a cup of tea, looking out at the sea. That's what you're going to learn to do now.

The Top Three Breakup Challenges

I put you on a frog fast back in the Introduction, but I bet some of you have been reading this book like some people read diet books, with one hand on the book and the other in a box of Oreos. Is a frog still in your life because:

1. You're still expecting a miracle.
   Girl Power Flash: I suspect that you will be able to walk on water before a frog turns into a prince.
2. You don't know how to end it.
   Girl Power Flash: Breakups are 99 percent attitude, preparation and delivery.
3. You're scared he'll raise a stink.
   Girl Power Flash: He can raise 700 kinds of stink, and you can still end it. If you follow the rules below, "swallowing" your frogs will be a cinch too.

The Right Breakup Attitude

Repeat after me: "My goal is to break up with him for good today, no matter what he says or does or how I feel about it, because he is a frog and I deserve better." This is your breakup mantra. If you memorize it, it will help you develop the attitude in the anonymous chain e-mail a friend forwarded me below, which sums up my frog breakup philosophy:

> Once upon a time a beautiful, independent, self-assured princess happened upon a frog in a pond. The frog said to the princess, "I was once a handsome prince until an evil witch put a spell on me.
>
> "One kiss from you and I will turn back into a prince and then we can marry, move into the castle with my mom, and you can prepare my meals, clean my clothes, bear my children, and forever feel happy doing so."
>
> That night, as the princess dined on the frog's legs in garlic butter, she laughed to herself and thought, "I don't fucking think so."

Now, couple the right attitude with this 3-prong breakup strategy—breakup prep, B-Day, and post-breakup pampering—and you'll be unstoppable.

Breakup Prep

1. *Review the carrots and sticks you created in Step 3.* Magnify the most motivating one over and over in your mind for a few days, and let it be your focal point on B-day.
2. *Initiate a sex moratorium and make yourself undesirable to him.* You must not under any circumstances have sex with anyone you're about to break up with. It will only cloud the issue and send mixed messages. Feel free to also customize any of the other break-up seeds that these women planted prior to B-Day:

❧ "I told Bud, my boyfriend of two months who was very squeamish about female problems, that he couldn't come over because I had to run out to the drugstore to pick up some Yeast Guard. He didn't talk to me for days and that made it easier to dump him."

❧ "My ex-jerk was an atheist, so I started spreading Jehovah's Witness pamphlets around my apartment and feigning interest in converting. I know I'm going to hell, but it totally turned him off."

❧ "I let myself go. I stopped shaving my legs or pits and wearing makeup, and I even began farting in front of him, without apologizing. By the end of the month he not only quit begging me not to move out, but he helped me rent a U-Haul."

3. *Take care of yourself.* Take your multivitamins; eat good food, exercise and rest well before B-Day. The better you feel about yourself, the better you'll feel about losing him.

4. *Plan out the breakup.* After you've decided when, where and how you're going to end it, visualize yourself doing it strongly, succinctly and successfully.

5. *Start thinking about what your life will be like without him.* What will you do with the time you used to spend with him? What will you tell your friends and family about the breakup? How will you celebrate? If you live together: Who will be moving out? What items will you have to replace (iron, coffee pot, stereo)? How will you have to adjust your budget to compensate for his absence? What items does he have that he may not give back once you break up with him?

6. *Enlist the help of a Frog-Recovery Sponsor.* Choose a girlfriend (or guy friend) who has been with you through thick and thin, who you know without a doubt wants you

to find the pot of gold at the end of the relationship rainbow, brief her about your goal of being frog-free, and ask for her support.

Caveats: She must love you enough to get in your face and say whatever she needs to say to help you protect yourself from frogs, like "No, no, no" and "Girl, are you craaaaaazy?" She must be able to discern when you are telling big, fat, hairy Frog Princess lies so you can hold on to your frog-of-the-moment. She must know your frog triggers and relationship fantasies by heart and be willing to interrogate you ruthlessly about breakup finality and future dates.

Her job: She is the one who's going to talk you down when you're about to jump back into the frog pond. If necessary, she will throw her body between you and Frog Boy, stare him down and spew out phrases like "If you want her, you'll have to come through me." If you call her and say nothing more than, "Help girl, I'm feeling weak," she'll read between the lines and immediately give you mind-to-mind resuscitation. And finally, if she catches you out in public getting cozy with the same Freddy Frog you supposedly dumped months ago, she will diplomatically pull you into the ladies room, cuff you, sneak you out the bathroom window, and force you to read your recovery pledge aloud until you're hoarse. Always think of her as your recovery ally, not the prude who's trying to spoil your fun. Accept the feedback she gives you without snipping or hissing. Remember, you want to lose the frogs, not your best girl.

B-Day

Your mission on this day is to break up with the frog in question immediately, forever. The only thing you should ever have to say to accomplish that is, "I don't want to see, talk to or hear from you ever again." I mean, that's a pretty all-inclusive statement that covers all forms of contact. What else is there? (Note: If you have children you will have to talk to and see him, but these are token visits—it's not like he's going to be in your bed again.) You don't have to offer a reason, or say you're sorry or give him a chance to have a turn, because he's a *frog* and your object is to get rid of him so you can have a healthier love life.

Managing Breakup Resistance

Of course, after you say this, he's likely to have the same look of horror that a man on life support would if he saw you getting ready to yank out the tube between him and the oxygen tank. And any frog worth his pedigree is then quickly going to (1) offer you money, jewelry, trips, or other expensive bribes, uh, gifts to reconsider; (2) hold one of your beloved possessions for ransom; (3) threaten to ruin your reputation; (4) implore your friends, family and maybe even God to get himself back in your good graces; (5) threaten to show up at your job or social events where he knows you're going to be; (6) beg; (7) cry.

Whatever your button is, however he's gotten you to overlook his warts and take his miserable butt back before, he's going to pull out all the stops to try to talk you down.

How do you ward off breakup resistance? "Stone cold is word," says 25-year-old Betty. "My ex said he couldn't breathe when I told him I was leaving him, so I pulled out my cell phone, dialed 9-1-1 and passed him the phone. I'll never forget the shocked look on his face." Here are a few more resolutions you should consider if you know the breakup is going to be challenging:

❧ **Be focused and clear.** It will keep you in control of the conversation.

❧ **Do not say anything that breeds confusion** or leaves room for makeup work or repair, like "Let's be friends" or "Maybe I just need a little space right now."

❧ **Do not let him talk to you after your normal bedtime,** or when you're bone tired, or allow him to go on for hours about the same thing. It's downright hypnotic. In fact, I hear it used to be a popular form of torture for use on prisoners of war.

❧ **Avoid physical contact.** No goodbye kisses, hugs or handholding.

❧ **Decide on a threshold for begging, whining and appeals.** Breakups are not hostage negotiations or peace summits. You do not have to stay until he agrees to let go of you. The more time you spend breaking up, the more likely you are to end up so disoriented from all the begging, whining and bribery that you might decide not to do it. So when you've had enough, go.

What If . . . ? Breakup Q & A

Don't spend a lot of time second-guessing yourself over whether or not you can salvage a frog-based relationship. What ifs can impede your breakup flow, so snap out of it. I've addressed some of the most popular pre-breakup What ifs below:

Q. What if he owes me money?
A. How much? Unless it's thousands and thousands of dollars, kiss the money goodbye. Let go of your CDs, books

and dishware he's borrowed too. Any collection efforts will keep you tied to him, thwarting your plan for a speedy getaway.

Q. What if he's fallen on hard times, like he's lost his job or a relative?

A. There's never going to be a good time in his life to get his walking papers. Refuse to let human sympathies get in the way of letting him go, so you can get on to something better.

Q. What if he says he's going to hurt himself if I leave him?

A. You are not responsible for an injury someone else decides to inflict upon himself. If he makes such a threat, tell someone who loves him (like his parents) about it and let them get him some help.

Q. What if he tries to make me feel guilty by saying I'm being too rash or unyielding?

A. Live with it. Who cares what he thinks of you as long as he's out of your life? I'd wager that you want him gone more than you want a congeniality award, right?

Q. What if I just haven't found the key to changing him into the man I want yet and what if I still love him?

A. Give up already. There's no shame in it. Don't take it personally if a frog remains a frog, that's his agenda. Cut your losses. So what if you don't get the blue ribbon at the Look What I Turned My Man Into Today contest, you'll have your freedom. Sometimes we do breeze in and out of relationships too quickly, but just as often, we commit too fast and stay way too long.

Which of these women do you think used the 3-prong breakup strategy I just described?

Breakup A: 26-year-old Lizzie

Lizzie, who had been the girlfriend of manic-depressive Frog Glen for fourteen months, tells this story: "When I told Glen I wanted to break up, he started to argue with me. Then he cried. Then he said that maybe we could make it if I started seeing his therapist too. I felt incredibly guilty and cheesy for abandoning him when he needed emotional support, so I told him that we could talk about it some more that night at my place. I mean it's the least I could do, we were together for over a year."

A week later she was fed up with his gloom-and-doom–like behavior all over again.

Breakup B: 33-year-old Abigail

Here's Abigail, who gave her boyfriend of three years the boot after his fifth DUI:

Frog: But I don't see why we can't give it another try. I'll stop drinking.

Abigail: Did you just hear the part about me not wanting to see you? Do you understand that this is it?

Frog: Can I call you tomorrow to talk about it some more?

Abigail: The phone? No, we will not be talking on the phone. And what else will we not be doing?

Frog: Seeing each other.

Abigail: That's right. Goodbye.

Post-breakup Pampering

If you guessed B, go get your Master Pampering list and treat yourself to something on it. In fact, pamper yourself after every breakup.

Frog or not, you're bound to be a little blue or lonely after B-Day, so, indulge yourself.

Pull-away Do's and Don'ts from a Breakup Queen

1. Do practice beforehand and compose answers for objections.
2. Do go for the jugular. Say whatever you think will make him let go.
3. Don't ever answer any trick questions that point to his goodness or your badness, like "Am I really that bad?" "Can't you give us another chance—you're not really going to be this heartless, are you?" "Don't you still love me, not even just a teensy-weensy little bit?"
4. Don't break up with him in pieces. Do it in one big chunk.
5. Do send a "Dear John" letter. It's a perfectly acceptable way of terminating a meaningless liaison. Who needs the potential drama of an unpleasant face-off?

Seven Frogs, Seven Breakup Boosters

Now that you have the tools for your breakup, here are seven common frog species to practice on. The basic skills that we've just reviewed should work for any of them, but I'll also point out a few other type-specific clinchers.

#1: Brute

Telltale traits: In addition to using his tongue to catch flies, Brute uses it to fling out putdowns and orders, and may have mistaken you in the past for a punching bag. In a word, he is nasty, cruel and ballistically inclined, a lot like the last short-tempered bad guy you saw in a shoot-em-up bang-bang movie.

Breaking Up with Brute:

- ✿ Strengthen your self-esteem by reading *David and Goliath* (the tale of a boy who takes on a mean giant with a slingshot and wins). Your slingshot is your faith in your new goal and yourself. Also, re-read the chapter on Living Juicy (Step 4) until you know how precious you are and how much you deserve someone who treats you like you're his queen. You have to treat yourself that way first.
- ✿ If physical violence is a major concern, break up by mail, phone or by proxy, or let your absence speak for itself, like Nerita. After her boyfriend beat her until she passed out, Nerita left home after he went to work the next day, with her 2-year-old daughter and the clothes on her back, and moved into a shelter 100 miles away from where she lived.
- ✿ Consult your local courthouse for details on applying for a restraining order, and then call a local domestic violence agency for more advice and counseling. As a general precaution, if Brute still comes around after you've done all of this, lock your doors, don't let him in and *call 9-1-1* whenever he shows up.

#2: Boy-Boy

Telltale traits: Boy-Boy is an immature, clingy Peter Pan type who might have a job that requires him to say, "Would you like fries with that?" or a figurehead position in the family business where he sits around making paper airplanes all day. If you've been bringing home the bacon and cooking it too, as well as cleaning up after him or being the only one to do anything that remotely resembles adult behavior, then chances are you've been with Boy-Boy.

Breaking Up with Boy-Boy:

- ⅋ Helpful Stick: Imagine an artist rendering a portrait of a pint-size version of Boy-Boy sucking his thumb and clinging to your leg with his other hand.
- ⅋ Talk over his head. Tell him you have to have a very serious ten-syllable operation or go away to some far off place like Guava Guava. (He'll never catch on that that's just a Snapple drink.)
- ⅋ Have an authority figure who loves him, like his mother, tell him. All the better if she thought you weren't good enough for her "little frog prince" in the first place.
- ⅋ You might have to reinforce this with him a few times, or have his mother do it. Like a child, he may return to his familiar habits and call you the next day, so it's important for him to have continual reinforcement until he remembers the new rules.
- ⅋ Do the unexpected if he throws a tantrum. Boy-Boy may cry, grab hold of your leg or arm, and throw the same wailing, high-pitched tantrum a 3-year-old would if she wanted a piece of candy in the grocery store. If he starts to cry, ignore him or walk away. If he starts whining, blow a whistle or clap out the theme song from *The Addams Family*. This will throw him off, and then you can get back to the breakup.

#3: Sneaky

Telltale traits: If he could have his way, polygamy would be legal. But since it's not, he's more likely to sneak off for mysterious, long trips to the gas station or laundromat. He usually has one arm around you, and the other one on his ever vibrating pager. If he's married (and you know it) you know the 101 reasons he can't leave her right away by heart—the kids, the house, his assets, etc. On the rare chance that he does leave her, your poor heart will be so weathered you won't even be able to relish your prize.

Breaking Up with Sneaky:

- ❧ Unfortunately, ugly, broke men cannot get away with offering themselves up as time-share men, so in all likelihood you will be sitting face-to-face with either a drop-dead gorgeous or rich man on B-Day. So, *minimize eye contact.* Look at your twiddling thumbs, or gaze at a painting on the wall while you're delivering your breakup speech. If he's Mr. Money Bags, it might also help to internally repeat the phrase, "I am not for sale."
- ❧ Helpful stick: Thirty-year-old Hazel says: "I thought about the time my married/separated boyfriend dialed his wife, from my house, and then passed me the phone, saying we'd have to work things out because he was just getting too stressed out from sneaking around behind her back." Helpful carrot: Think about purring in the arms of a man who cherishes you and you alone.
- ❧ Use visual aids. If you have any snapshots someone took of him having dinner with another woman, spread them out on the table. If you have any phone bills with the same recurring long-distance number, add them to the

incriminating collage. You could also surprise him with an I-know-what-you've-been-doing-you-sneak basket filled with suspicious panties, bras, lipstick-stained shirts and love letters.

#4: High-N-Low

Telltale Traits: Basically, we're talking Jekyll/Hyde syndrome here, which may or may not be drug or alcohol induced. High-N-Low is up one day, down the next, often unduly influenced by life's normal woes, like bad traffic, bad weather and basketball game scores. His best hope for a turnaround is under the professional tutelage of a drug intervention specialist or a licensed counselor.

Breaking Up with High-N-Low:

- ⚘ Helpful carrot: See yourself swinging in a peaceful hammock with an emotionally stable man.
  Helpful stick: Picture High-N-Low embarrassing you or your child at a public event, like what happened to 34-year-old Geneva. Daddy Dearest came staggering down the aisle in the middle of his daughter's dance recital slurring out something that sounded vaguely like, "There's my baby girl." Then he bumped into the principal and threw up all over him, while their hysterical daughter ran off the stage.
- ⚘ Put the onus on him by verbalizing your displeasure that he's burdened your relationship with his substance addiction or mental problems. You might say something like what 39-year-old Charlee told her ex: "I'm sick of going to Al-Anon with you. I don't have a drinking problem, you do."

#5: *Fossil*

Telltale traits: At heart, Fossil is an old-fashioned fifties man who likes his women barefoot and pregnant, mousy and obedient. He is the spirit of your great-grandfather trapped in a new millennium and may have even publicly remarked that it's a damn shame women have the right to work outside the home and vote when they were born to cook and clean. N.O.W. who? When he gets home, he wants to know when dinner is going to be ready and whether or not you've starched his shirt for the next day, even if you just beat him in the door by 10 minutes.

Breaking Up with Fossil:

- ❧ Start doing things a couple of weeks before B-Day that will let him know that you aren't a June Cleaver clone. If you do cook regularly, stop for a week, and when he asks where dinner is, say you were wondering the same thing. If you pick up after him, wash the dishes, vacuum, and generally do the bulk (if not all) of the household chores, take a vacation from that too.
- ❧ As a motivating carrot, imagine yourself with a man who can quickly define "teamwork," "progressive thinking" and "equal partnership" and enjoys pitching in to do all of the things it takes to keep a household running.
- ❧ As a motivating stick, picture Fossil handcuffing and gagging you, and dragging you to an equally Fossil-like mad scientist so he can turn you into a Stepford Wife.

#6: Icy

Telltale traits: With Icy, you might need to dress in layers in the house, because he comes with his own wind chill factor. At least the Tin Man in *The Wizard of Oz* wanted a heart. Icy would rather have another snow cone. It's no wonder that you've been having a recurring dream about sticking him in the oven with the pot roast to see if that would thaw him out emotionally.

Breaking Up with Icy:

- ❧ Icy is a fairly easy breakup. Stick to the basic script I mentioned earlier. It's cut and dried and to the point, and that's the way Icy likes it.
- ❧ If you need more of a stick motivation, think about the last time you reached for him for warmth and tenderness and wound up with frost-bitten hands, like 38-year-old Dorothy: "I had a mastectomy and I was lying there in my bed, just home from the hospital, crying, mourning my lost breast, and he wouldn't even hold me. Not only that, he eventually stared me down and ordered me to get over myself. As soon as I could, I drove down to the nearest attorney and filed for divorce, replaying that scene the whole time."

#7: Mismatch

Telltale traits: With Mismatch, it's mostly a compatibility issue. He's nothing special, nothing awful. He's just the yin to your yang, the water to your fire, the earth to your sky. He's undoubtedly nice and doting, but as far as common ground goes, forget it. For example, he's a couch potato; you're a marathon

runner. He's crazy about basketball; you think it's a mindless social phenomenon. You're active in your church; he's still trying
to figure out if he's technically an agnostic or an atheist. If he
found the right woman who had similar values and personality
traits, his name would be King.

Breaking Up with Mismatch:

- Employ a little more heart and gentility with Mismatch,
  unless he puts up resistance. Then you'll have to cut
  him off at the knees. You can tell him you think he's
  wonderful, just not *your* kind of wonderful. You can also
  imply that it's more of a benefit to him to break up with
  you. You are unworthy. Use phrases like, "You deserve a
  woman who adores you," and "I see myself dancing at
  your wedding to a woman who is more in tune with your
  needs."
- As for carrots, picture him with his ideal woman and you
  with your ideal man.

If the frog you want to break up with doesn't quite fit into any
of these categories, but he's real close, he may be a transitional
frog. Working off the warts, so to speak. I've got five words
about transitional frogs: Wait until they cross over.

Now for a quick pop quiz. As quickly as possible, match the
frogs in Column B with the descriptions in Column A.

Column A   **Column B**

1. You overhear a man in line buying concert   a. Brute
   tickets say he has to swing by his mother's
   afterward to pick up his laundry and make   b. Boy-Boy
   himself a bologna and pickle sandwich.

2. You board a day cruise and a man whistles   c. Sneaky
   at you from the top deck of the boat. You
   climb the stairs only to find his wife staring   d. High-N-
   you down like you're the thing from the deep.   Low

3. You walk into a club just in time to spot a
   man grab another woman by the hair and   e. Fossil
   pull her out onto the dance floor.

4. You're sitting in a movie theater watching a   f. Icy
   real tearjerker like *Love Story*, and the guy
   beside you, who apparently has no tear   g. Mismatch
   ducts, looks at his watch and asks if it's
   almost over.

5. You're at a wine-tasting class and there's one
   man in the circle whom the instructor has to
   continually remind to pass the wine bottles.
   He also gulps instead of sipping.

6. You're at the Laundromat and every time you
   go out to feed the meter the creep in the
   cowboy boots turns the Laundromat radio
   station from R & B (which you love) to
   country (which you hate).

7. You're at a PTA meeting to gather ideas for
   increasing attendance at girls' sporting
   events, and the guy behind you wearing
   brown polyester pants with a bowtie pipes in
   with "Why are girls playing basketball and
   soccer anyway? Can't they just be cheerleaders?"

Here are the answers: 1. b 2. c 3. a 4. f 5. d 6. g 7. e
If you got less than five of them right, then before you go any further, carefully review the seven frog types.

Indications the Breakup Didn't Take

Try as you may, even though it seemed like you executed the perfect split script, breakups do not take the first time with every frog. Take 26-year-old Brittany, for instance. She broke up with Alan on a Tuesday. She was very clear, very purposeful, and she returned his CDs and told him to keep her Victoria's Secret panties because she wasn't going to come over to his house to pick them up (at his ransom-like suggestion). He called her on Wednesday to see if she'd changed her mind about coming to collect her under-things. She said "no" and hung up. On Thursday, he invited her to a picnic lunch at the lake with their favorite couple friends. Stunned, she said, "How thick are you? Didn't you hear what I said about breaking up with you?" She hung up the phone and sat there scratching her head. Here are some other indications he's still holding on:

1. In addition to nonchalant phone calls, he also drops by your home or office, often with gifts.
2. His friends call you to try to patch things up.
3. He still refers to you as his girlfriend to mutual friends.

If you have a clinging frog, try these strategies until he gives up:

🐸 Repeat your breakup instructions immediately every time he calls or sees you, and have him repeat what you said back to you. It will help it sink in best if you say exactly the same thing each time, with the same firm tone.

&. Contact his wife/boss/parents/friend (whoever will be most ashamed of him and intercede) and tell them you broke up with him and he's still bothering you. This is a little extreme, but if he still makes himself a nuisance, try this line, "If you don't leave me alone, I'll get a restraining order." Note: If you threaten it, you'll have to do it, and you will need some recent evidence of bodily harm or harassment.

&. If you don't have grounds for a restraining order, rework your life so that him catching a glimpse of you would be like seeing the next eclipse. What he doesn't see, he'll learn to live without.

Are You Over Him?

Maybe he's let go and you haven't. After she broke up with her ex-boyfriend Tommy, 33-year-old Emerald called him a week later to reiterate her parting words: "It's not healthy for me to be around you anymore. As soon as I'm over you, I'll call you." Surely, he was sitting there with the same, "Huh?" look on his face that I had when she shared this with me. This clearly goes under the category of things that make you sound dumb and pitiful. So does 42-year-old Amber's rationalization to her mother (her frog recovery sponsor) that she just wanted to call Jed, her abusive ex-husband, to see if he was okay. I told a friend who wanted me to do a drive-by to check out her ex-husband's new love nest with his girlfriend that it shouldn't make any difference in her life whether he's living in a palace or a peapod if she wasn't his honey anymore. If you want to let go of a frog, let him go. Don't make up bogus reasons to call or see him, or put anyone else up to it either.

These tips will help you shake off heartbreak, when and if it comes:

1. *Set a time limit to be heartbroken.* It could be a day for every month you've known him, thirty days, or some other short, finite period of time. When it's over, so ends your breakup drama. Are you with me?
2. *Mourn your loss.* Whether he let go or you did, a loss is still a loss and you have the right to mourn it. So, boo-hoo, listen to sad love songs like *Unbreak My Heart* (Toni Braxton) and *How Can I Breathe Without You?* (LeAnn Rimes), fawn longingly over his pictures and post pitiful long-suffering messages on cyber-breakup chat rooms until you've gotten it out of your system.
3. *Vent.* If you have unresolved anger about your breakup, get it out of your heart by (a) pounding on a pillow or a punching bag and pretending it is your ex's face; (b) burning his pictures, letters, or paper mementos; (c) screaming; (d) writing a nasty, scathing letter to him. (Do not deliver the letter, and honor the time limit you set in number 1.) Here's a letter that 26-year-old Alyssa wrote after she broke up with Frog Roger:

Dear Loser,

I hope the baby bald spot on the top of your head that I pretended not to notice when I looked down on your head since *I am still taller than you*, doubles in size every forty-eight hours until *you are completely bald*. Not that you don't already look like Bozo the Clown. I hope the bimbo that you're with now can deal with your cheesy performance in bed too. And, since you believe in reincarnation, I hope you come back as a worm, and that some little kid decides to burn you to a crisp with a magnifying glass one summer. *You freaking jerk!*

4. *Learn, Forgive, Release.* In martial arts there's a tradition of bowing to your opponent before and after a match as a sign of respect and appreciation, for without them you would not have a chance to strengthen your skills and achieve mastery. Heartbreak happens, but why not think of your heartbreakers as teachers who have come into your life under the guise of romance to teach you something that might not even be about love? Whenever your heart is broken in two, search for the lesson and the blessing, forgive him and then release. *Do not move on before you find the blessing,* not even if your only blessing was simply that things weren't even worse.

5. *Pamper yourself.* When I was helping a 20-year-old friend recover from her first heartbreak over a guy she'd been dating briefly until she caught him flirting with another girl, I drew her a bubble bath, lit a candle, made her some tea and told her, "This is the way you get over a guy. With quiet dignity and lots of pampering." Break out your bubble bath and your candles, put on your warm fuzzy slippers and make yourself a cup of tea too.

6. *Take a romance sabbatical.* As a longtime yoga enthusiast and former type A personality, I have often struggled with the pose savasanah, which is one of the most important poses in yoga because it is the position of repose. At the end of a yoga session, after all the twisting and stretching, your job is to lie flat on your back like a corpse, resting and renewing. Whenever you have a broken heart, savasanah. It will give you a chance to replenish your spirit, regroup and enjoy your single solitude. It will also reduce the likelihood of short-sighted rebound relationships.

7. *After you've felt the pain, move beyond it.* Sufi poet Kahlil Gibran once said, "And could you keep your heart

in wonder at the daily miracles of your life, your pain would not seem less wondrous than your joy. And you would accept the seasons of your heart, even as you have always accepted the seasons that pass over your fields." Give yourself time to mourn, vent, write nasty letters (that you don't mail), pamper, extract the lessons, and the blessings and then pick up the pieces of your heart and get back to living juicy. Love comes again if your heart is open to it.

Let's Not Be Friends

One of the surest ways to keep frogs in your midst is to end romantic involvement and continue to dangle friend strings in front of them. Most guys don't understand the "let's just be friends" philosophy. What they hear when you say this is, "Maybe I'll have another chance with her one day. In the meantime, I can still stay close." And frankly, if he's a frog, why do you want him as your buddy?

Frog Cleaning, Phase Two

Now that you've broken up, it's time for phase two of the purge, which is to get rid of everything you can that reminds you of him—clothes, pictures, trinkets, knickknacks, the works. After you collect these items, I'm not advocating creating a bonfire (unless, of course, you have a permit) or a yard sale (unless you could use a little extra cash). But powerful sentimental anchors live in inanimate objects that might weaken your resolve to give a frog up permanently, so you've got to get them out of your home. Why do you think when you hold an object that someone gave you, and they're nowhere to be seen, you think of them? It's the same for you and Froggie; even without his presence, if you have subtle, or not so subtle reminders of him, it will take you longer to let him go in your psyche (where it really counts). For example, here's what I did a few days after my ex-husband moved out:

1. *Clothing:* Got half a dozen jumbo trash bags and dumped all of his favorites into them. By the time I was through, I had about three outfits left, five pairs of bloomer cotton panties, two sports bras and a pair of shoes.

2. *Furniture and knickknacks:* Got rid of his ashtrays, and our sectional couch (which he lazed around on all the time) one section at a time.

3. *Pictures:* Tucked the pictures of him and my daughter away in her room, and I burned the photos of him and me together.

4. *Hair:* Had my shoulder-length hair chopped down to less than an inch for the new me who was rising out of the ashes of a disastrous relationship.

5. *Furniture (part 2):* Whatever I couldn't replace right away, I used differently. For instance, I rearranged my bedroom furniture, and eventually bought a futon—the type of bed he would never have slept on, but I love.

What You Can Do to Purge

Get rid of ALL things that remind you of him the most, unless:

1. It has utilitarian value. House, car, tools, electronic equipment, furniture, etc.

2. You have a child together. Offer to store them for your child in a keepsake trunk.

Anything else should be trashed, burned, donated or sold. In the spirit of reducing waste, cut up any shirts or soft clothing and use them as dusting or dish rags.

Firing Frog's Family and Friends Too

"I was seeing a guy who wanted to marry me, and then went 'weird' all of a sudden. His parents still call me and say things like 'we still pray about things with you and XXXX. We have always hoped that you two would get married.' "

Mutual friends and family can keep you entangled and what you need right now is freedom, girl, so cut those cords. Unless of course you have had children with him. Then you remain civil and connected because of the children, but you do not over-extend yourself like 30-year-old Angel, who sent postcards, electric bill money and a plane ticket to her Brute boyfriend's mother, who often still referred to him as her little darling.

Gag Orders

Raise your hand if you're one of those women who spend about just as much time talking about your ex as you did when you were with him. This is another form of hanging on to him. The more you talk about him (even if you're saying nasty things), the more you keep him alive. You should not spend five minutes rehashing old times with old frogs because you have other things to do. Review your Living Juicy exercises and ask your friends to interrupt you or change the subject when you bring him up too frequently.

Recovery Exercises

1. Plan your breakup strategy.
2. Get a frog recovery sponsor. Tell her about your breakup and your recovery objectives.
3. Start your purge.

R & R Journal exercise: Save one picture of each of the frogs you've shared your life with and create a Frog Album. Beside each picture, list his frog type (i.e., Boy-Boy, Sneaky, Fossil, etc.).

Prince Rob

Thirty-four-year-old hairstylist Rob Daniels loves doing the unexpected when it comes to romancing his 23-year-old wife, Anitra. So far, though, their wedding has been his best surprise.

Three years ago Anitra transferred to Seattle Pacific University to be closer to her boyfriend, Rob. At Sea-Tac airport, when she stepped off the plane and into his open arms she was wearing a special dress as he requested because she thought they were going out to dinner. But little did she know that Rob had spent the last two weeks planning a surprise wedding, complete with a wedding party who sat waiting in adjacent terminals with newspapers covering their faces until he popped the question.

In an instant, he dropped to one knee and asked for her hand in marriage. "Yes," she said as she stooped down to kiss him lovingly. When they were both back on their feet, a minister appeared before her. "Now?" she asked. But before he could answer, one of the wedding party screamed out, "You're getting married, girl!"

"It's kind of funny," he continued with misty eyes, "about a year after I met her she said I was going to marry her, but I didn't believe it. And there we were."

"Rob is still full of surprises," says Anitra, "and he's so thoughtful, he always puts me and the kids first. Yesterday we went to the mall to get something for him and he saw me looking at a dress and he said, 'Let's get it, and I'll come back and get my stuff next time.' He has a strict schedule at work, too, that revolves around us. He often leaves early to be with us and goes back to clean up his shop early the next day when we're asleep."

And you can bet that surprise is still a big theme of their marriage. This Valentine's Day, while they were talking in bed in the wee hours of the morning, he pulled out a jewelry store flyer and pointed to a ring and said, "Do you like this?" When she said yes, he pulled the ring out of his pajama pocket and slipped it onto her finger.

STEP 6

Protect Your Heart from Future Frog Invasions

Lesson: Once you've given old frogs the boot, new temptations may hop around outside your cottage, croaking loudly to test your resolve. Take all the preventative measures you can to keep your heart from becoming a target for another froggy takeover.

Affirmations

1. Keeping frogs away will give me more opportunities for joy.
2. I am the queen of repelling.
3. I know how to use my body, mind, and spirit for repelling.

Whew! Now that you've booted old frogs out of your life, you'd probably like nothing more than to never have to deal with another frog again. The bad news: There will always be frogs, my dear. At the grocery store, the movie theater, the bank, the park—everywhere. The good news: If you equip yourself with the right tools you can instantly construct an invisible barrier between you and unwanted frogs.

Who Do You Want to Repel?

Basically, Type I and Type II frogs. The Type I frog will be easiest to recognize. (If you can get him in a good light and pull back one of his ears, you might even spot a faint F.R.O.G. stamp.) If he's one of the seven frog species outlined in the previous step, after brief mindful observation of his behavior and language, you *will* know. In fact, for the next month whenever you encounter them don't be surprised if you are struck with a sudden, overwhelming urge to smugly holler out, "Brute," "Boy-Boy," "Icy," etc.

A Type II frog, on the other hand, will reveal himself more slowly, like a mystery novel. He may very well look and sound like a prince at first (and maybe second) take, but he won't hold up for long. Later on in Step 8, I'll teach you scanning techniques to chop your reading time in half. For now though, let's get you up to speed on basic repelling with the Type I frogs. Any time you encounter a frog, practice the following repelling techniques.

Cut Them Off at the Pass

A lot of men have the mistaken perception that whenever you're in a public place you're fair game for a pick-up line. Your task is to create the perception that you are not. With stranger frogs, you've got the biggest advantage. They don't know your triggers, they don't know your history, and they also don't know the type of whopping lies you might be willing to tell to get them away from you. Forget about honesty. I wish I could tell you that the truth will set you free from frogs, but it's more likely to backfire on you. Take 23-year-old Lily, for example, who told a frog who hit on her at a club that she didn't date smokers. He promptly put his cigarette out, popped in a breath mint and said, "There. Now can we talk?" And there's 28-year-old Blanche, who thought she'd stopped a solicitous frog dead in his tracks by mentioning that she'd seen him kissing another woman minutes earlier. "Oh, baby," he crooned, "she didn't mean anything to me. But *you*, you could take me to the next level." Truth rarely works with frogs, as you may have seen when you were conducting your breakups in the last step, so do not feel the least bit guilty about spinning the quickest tale that comes to mind. It's not like you'll ever have to go to any of these frogs for blood or kidney donations or a raise, so have fun with it. My creative repelling license has taken the form of pretending that (1) English was not my native language; (2) I was married (for years I've worn a garnet ring on my ring finger—my daughter's birthstone—when I know I'm going to be in high-frog-traffic areas); (3) I was newly pregnant and extremely nauseous.

Time for a quiz:

What if a guy with a beer belly, who was just arguing with a police officer about being double-parked outside the movie theater, heads your way. Do you:

a. Stand there nervously until he makes it over to you and begrudgingly agree to sit with him?
b. Make a dash to the bathroom, and then claim the seat farthest away from him and put your coat and assorted items in the chairs to the east, west, north and south of you?

And another:

What if you're at the opera, and the guy in the seat next to you, who looks and sounds very much like a frog and keeps shifting in his chair and smiling suggestively at you, eventually whispers, "Do you have a boyfriend?" Do you:

a. Politely smile back at him, and say "No"?
b. Turn to fully face him like he has a personal problem, and fling out a slightly abrasive "Yes!" and stare straight ahead for the duration of the performance?

The B's have it. If you don't engage frogs, all roads lead nowhere. Here's a roundup of more repelling basics to cut pestering frogs off at the pass:

❧ **Body Repelling.** You've heard the saying "actions speak louder than words." Well, if a frog approaches you, let your body repel him first. You know how to reel a guy in, don't you? A little coy, inviting smile, a little batting of the eyelashes, a little hoisting up of your twin peaks, a little leaning into him if you get the chance. To cast frogs out do a reversal, and swing the other way until you put them off enough so they'll move on. Start with (1) frowning; (2) folding your arms; (3) tapping your feet in a manner that in no uncertain terms implies that if they don't wrap up their come-on line so you can just get back to standing there without them, you're going to lose it; (4) turning your back on them; (5) taking two steps back; (6) rolling your eyes or looking off into the distance; (7) scrunching up your nose like you smell musty feet. When all else fails, nothing says "go away" like walking away while he's talking.

❧ **Tongue Repelling.** One of my friends has the following recording on his outgoing mail, "Hello, you've reached the so-and-so residence. If you are a solicitor, hang up and never call here again." After that there are numbers that you can press to reach either him or his wife in the residence, but phone peddlers quickly get the message to scratch his number off their prospect list. When repelling frogs, you must also aim for the jugular and say the thing you know he doesn't want to hear; the thing that nips any possibility of a long, hopeful, drawn-out conversation in the bud. Like these phrases: "I'm not even remotely interested"; "Go away and leave me alone"; "I've got pepper spray." If the situation requires something more, here are my favorite repel lines used by the women I interviewed to ping frogs in the past:

- "I told him I had a nervous condition that often intensified when I was in close proximity to anyone who'd been drinking that tended to make me violent."
- "I asked him if he wanted to go to the Gay Pride parade that weekend with my girlfriend and me."
- "I mentioned that I was a black belt."
- "When he put his hand on my leg under the dinner table at a friend's party, I said as loud as I could, 'Is that your hand on my leg, Ryan?!' "
- "I told him I had fibroid tumors (I don't), described them in great detail and then asked if he knew of any good OB-GYNs."
- "I asked him if male pattern baldness ran in his family (he was starting to thin just a little around the crown)."
- "I told him my wrestler boyfriend, Ivan Ragotulli, told me to page him if anyone bothered me. (Ivan's my pretend boyfriend. Sometimes I want to crack up because it even sounds like a fake name.)"

❧ *Psychic Repelling.* I once had a friend named Mercedes who enjoyed going out to nightclubs to dance to top 40. Knowing dance clubs are big frog pits, I found it curious that she was never really hounded by any of them although she's just gorgeous. When I asked her for her repelling secret, she said she cast an imaginary circle of white light around her so that no ordinary frog could cross. Sure enough, I went out with her one night and watched her in action. What was so funny was that when men got within a few feet I saw this weird look on their faces like the one I once saw on a German shepherd when I blew a dog whistle. They wanted to talk to her, but for some inexplicable reason that they couldn't quite put their finger on, the closer they got, the harder it became to reach her. Want to use your psychic repelling powers to keep frogs at bay too? Try these:

a. Imagine a protective bubble around you that extends out twenty feet in all directions.
b. If you see a frog coming your way, start repeating internally "I am immune to frogs," or simply "Stay away, stay away, stay away."
c. At the beginning of the day, visualize yourself going through the day without any encounters of a froggy kind.

Body/Tongue/Psychic Repelling in Action

Yesterday as I was entering a store, a man hopped over and croaked out, "Sweet Jesus! An angel right here on earth. Would you bless me with your phone number?" First, since he was blocking my path, I folded my arms (body repelling) and asked my daughter, who was with me, what she wanted for dinner, without even acknowledging him. "I cook! And I'm good with kids," he said, winking at my daughter, who was eyeballing him like he was a diseased talking sewer rat.

"I need you to move right now. I don't want to talk to you, and I'm definitely not giving you my phone number." (Tongue repelling.) He didn't budge, and he stood there grinning at me like I'd change my mind any minute until I suddenly pointed to nothing in the distance and said, "Would you look at that?" When he turned, I grabbed Esprit and rushed into the store. (Tongue, followed by body repelling.)

When we were finished shopping I thought he might be waiting for us, so I told Esprit that we were going to put up our psychic cloaking device (this is very *Star Trek* chic) by repeating "Frogs away, frogs away, frogs away," and sneak out the other door and beat it to our car. Sure enough, when we drove out of the parking lot, we spotted him looking puzzled by the door.

If a Brick-like Frog Has You Cornered

1. Send him on a wild goose chase. Politely ask him to get you a glass of water, or a pen with green ink, or a Japanese dictionary. Don't be there when he gets back.
2. Grab on to the first person you know who you think can save you and bring them into your conversation, and then offer to go somewhere with them, even if it's just outside for air or to point out the night stars.
3. Start coughing or hacking, or faint.
4. Take a really long time to answer his questions. It sometimes takes one friend of mine a few minutes to answer a question he doesn't really want to answer. He says he's doing an internal check to make sure what he says is really true, but sometimes it just drives me to the living edge.

So Can You Ever Be Friendly to Strangers?

Yes and no. Yes, you can say hello, talk about how nice the weather is and exchange pleasant small talk while you're standing in line at the post office, but the absolute second you hear a "rrribbit," fly into repel mode. This was hard for me at first because I'm a very friendly person for the most part. But with frogs I've learned that anything that can be taken as an invitation to romance will be, and sometimes this includes civil chit chat about nothing I'll ever remember. Let me tell you about four glaring reminders from my past:

- ⁀ *Outdoor concert, 1999.* A friend and I attended a summer concert at the zoo, and I'd said hi to a few guys in passing because they said hi to me, but when my friend went for lemonade, she confessed that one of them had followed her and asked if I was single, and she—forgetting all about good second-hand repelling—said yes and agreed to pass on his phone number to me. "Tell her to please call me. Tell her I really like her aura, and that I bet we have a lot in common." Again, all I said was hi as I walked in the other direction, chatting with my friend the whole time.
- ⁀ *Parent night, 1998.* I struck up a conversation with the father of one of my daughter's friends over the punch bowl. As near as I can remember, I smiled and said, "How are you? I'm Esprit's mom. Do you know where the girls went?" But after school the next day, Esprit reported that this egomaniac, thinking we'd had some enchanted moment, had told his daughter I'd made a pass at him.
- ⁀ *Work, 1997.* A married co-worker, whom I'll call David,

and I started a small creative writer's e-mail group at work. He, I, and three other writers exchanged mostly poems and short-short fiction. I sent out one poem about my daughter's first steps, but instead of critiquing it like everyone else, David sent me (and me alone) a steamy poem entitled "First Date." I fired off another about my fascination with the beach, and he sent one (to me alone again) called "Sexual Passion." (Next, I sent a short story about a bitter woman who dreamed about hosting her own exposé TV show to publicly humiliate men who cheated on their wives. Needless to say, he backed off for a few weeks.)

❧ *School, 1996:* Once I heard a husky voice calling my name in the campus bookstore. When I turned, this veritable stranger was lustfully giving me the once over. I gave him a blank look, thought maybe I'd seen him as a bank clerk or a waiter, but didn't know him. His version of our acquaintance was that we had mutually admired each other over our computer screens in a COBOL class some eight years before. Suddenly, it hit me. He was the one who always strolled in late for class, or skipped altogether, and then had the most creative excuses in the world. *I mean, this guy was good.* One day he told the instructor his 3-year-old daughter was having a past-life memory of being tortured as a P.O.W. so he could retake the midterm. He even cried. I almost believed him. He re-created our history too. I remembered speaking to him twice: to tell him to pass the assignment sheets and to stop looking at my paper during a test. What did he think, that after some time, I'd forgotten what really happened and he could fill in the blanks at his leisure?

Repelling Frogs You've Been With

The first set of repelling strategies was for frogs you don't know who instantly fit into the Type I category you learned about in the previous step. (Brute, Boy-Boy, etc.) This set is for Type II frogs you've dated, lived with or married who turned out to be surprise frogs, and are still holding on to you, milking their prior knowledge of your soft spots, triggers and relationship fantasies for all they're worth. Maybe every time you turn around, you see his begging-for-another-chance face. Maybe he checks in with you every few months with the same regularity as the charities that call to see if you have any donations for the truck that's going to be in your area. Whether you've had one night with him or a decade, if the breakup techniques in the previous chapter didn't take, you're going to have to step up your repelling efforts until it disrupts his homing frequency. Here's a real-world repelling prescription.

Thirty-three-year-old Kay says of Frog Jimmy, "He called Friday night on his cell phone to say that it was the tenth anniversary of the day we met. I swallowed hard and all the love came rushing back in a flood of memories. He still knew my favorite color, how I made him vow that we'd never fight on Fridays, and that I loved pastrami sandwiches and banana splits without the ice cream. 'Has some lucky guy taken you off the market yet?' he asked. When I told him no he wanted to know if I still had the black lace thong panties he bought me, and boldly came right out and said that he'd like to see me in them when he came to town next weekend on business. Then I asked the hard question, the reason I'd broken up with him two years ago, 'Are you still married to *her*?' And although he threw out the same tired rationalization he'd used the night of our breakup—the kids are almost grown, I'll leave her then, you know I still need you and I miss you—I let him come. I was even wearing the panties when I opened the door."

Rx for Kay: First, Kay needs to purge her home of those thong panties and anything else that serves as strong anchors to Jimmy. Then she should do the following: (1) block his cell phone number; (2) hang up on him immediately if he calls her from anywhere else, after instructing him to never call again; (3) offer motivating negative consequences, like threatening to contact his wife.

The Last Froggy Temptation of Nailah

I want to tell you the story of how I got over Hunter, who could turn me into mush within three seconds with his big, dreamy eyes, Mr. Universe body and gut-busting jokes. He could also sing every ballad Luther Vandross has ever recorded almost as well as Luther Vandross himself. He was a gourmet cook, a poet, an entrepreneur and songwriter, and I was in deep without even having slept with him. Until the day I walked in on him unexpectedly at his studio singing the same song he said he wrote for me to a woman he quickly tried to introduce as "his really good old friend" after I did a hasty about-face. I hurried home, cursing all men, and blocked his number as soon as I deleted the dozen messages he'd left when I was en route to my home. So he called from other numbers, night after night, leaving incredibly long, silky apologies. For almost a month, he sent flowers, which I dropped off at a senior's home up the street, and I didn't call him back. I'm still not sure how I pulled that off other than just knowing that if I ever talked to him again, I'd lose face with the part of me that was trying desperately not to be a Frog Princess anymore.

After a year, when I moved to be closer to work, and changed my phone number, I thought I was finally free of him. But one day when I listened to my voice mail messages, I heard his familiar silky voice serenading me with *Here and Now*. I felt myself melting. I felt my hand gravitating toward the receiver. And then I reached out with my other hand and pulled it back. It turns out an old schoolmate of ours—whom I lectured severely after his call—gave him my new phone number. He left two messages every day for a little over a month. Because of him, I became a very fast draw on my voice mail delete button.

Recovery Exercises

1. Meet with your frog recovery sponsor to devise a personalized set of body, tongue and psychic repelling strategies.
2. Go to a public place and practice repelling the first three frogs who approach you.

R & R Journal exercise: Make a list of three people you know who are good at repelling annoying people and write down how they do it.

Prince Kai

Malia, a 38-year-old journalist, has been dating 32-year-old postal worker Kai for a year. She tells this story:

I'd always thought there was something weird about having a younger lover. And I doubt I'll ever feel that way again, even if our relationship flops. So far it's the best relationship I've ever had with another human being, and I love him.

My hairdresser Tom introduced us last year at the salon. I liked his rich chocolate skin, his slender body, his smile, and his easy laugh then, but when Tom told me how old Kai was, I lost interest. Then I saw him at a Christmas party months later and he asked me out. When I told him I didn't date younger men, he said he didn't want to be prejudged for being my junior and that age was just a number. "Why don't you just pretend I'm five and a half years older than you. Would it be okay for us to go out then?" After he said that I realized how ridiculous I was being, but I still didn't know how he'd react to me having a daughter. So I told him I was a single mom, and all he asked was if she was well behaved and if he could pay for the babysitter when we went out.

There's nothing we didn't talk about on the first date. I really can't believe I was thinking this, but I was surprised a postal worker could be so smart and so interesting. After about an hour I quickly forgot that he was in diapers when I started first grade.

STEP 7

Raise Your Standards

Lesson: If you want better men, you have to acquire better tastes. This step will teach you how to hoist your expectations and standards for choosing men to a new all-time high, and learn to like it.

Affirmations

1. I love having the best of the best.
2. The best is just right for me.
3. I take pride in letting good standards overflow into every area of my life.

One day Joy was walking through the forest when she came across a little cottage. She was so thirsty that she knocked on the door, hoping the kindly resident would offer her a glass of Evian water. When no one answered, she invited herself in and, unfortunately, had to settle for tap. While she was filling her glass, she noticed a tiny rose-colored plaque on the wall with the words "A princess must always marry a prince. Yours may be closer than you think, so make yourself at home." As Joy had already broken and entered, she didn't think there'd be much more harm in taking a look around to see if her prince was really in the house. So she went to the living room.

On the sofa sat the handsomest man she'd ever seen, but he barely looked up from the wrestling match he was watching to demand that she fix him a sandwich. Joy backed quickly out of the room without asking if he wanted turkey or tuna. "Too bossy. The nerve," she whispered as she headed upstairs.

She walked into an elegant bedroom just in time to see a tanned man coming out of the shower with only a towel wrapped around his waist. "There you are, darling," he said to her as she melted. But then the phone rang, and he quickly excused himself to the bathroom with the cordless, saying it was his brother. "Too sneaky," said Joy, who had clearly heard a woman's voice on the other end of the line.

She went back downstairs to the kitchen for another glass of water, and much to her surprise, there stood a candlelit table set for two. "I hope you like Szechwan chicken," said the smiling, dimpled man who appeared and seated her. "This one is just right," she thought to herself, as she began to eat the three-course home-cooked Chinese dinner he'd prepared for her. It was so wonderful that she ate it slowly, enjoying each bite, smiling back at him all the while.

We've spent the last few chapters clearing froggy cobwebs out of your brain, and hopefully you've broken up with all of the frogs who used to be part of your life. Now it's time to teach you to choose the best man. No more Boy-Boys, no more Brutes, no more High-N-Lows. You can learn to raise your standards far more easily than you realize by adopting the rules that follow.

Knowing What You Need

Before you permanently raise your standards for choosing romantic partners, you'll need three things:

First, you need to know what "better" is.

Second, you need to really believe you deserve "better."

Third, you need to globally integrate your new belief into your lifestyle.

A Basic Standards Test

Pretend for a few minutes that you are a guest on the old T.V. show *The Dating Game*, except you have a full frontal view of each bachelor in sequential order, and you get to ask each five questions. After interviewing a bachelor you can agree to go on a date with him, but if you do, you will not get to meet any of the others who could be better, or could be worse. Which bachelor would you choose?

Bachelor #1 is ten inches taller or shorter than you like, and has some other physical feature that makes him resemble your version of a swamp thing (for me, that would be a pudgy man with a squeaky voice and without facial hair). You can never imagine holding hands with him, let alone kissing him or snuggling with him in your birthday suit. And who knows if you'll ever be able to have a decent conversation with him the way he keeps fumbling through your questions. Does he have a hearing problem, is he conjuring up a lie, or is he really that slow? In short, the only thing the two of you have in common is that you are both breathing.

Bachelor #2 is pleasantly nondescript. He's not physically repulsive, but he's not drop-dead gorgeous either. You would probably walk right by him on the street tomorrow without even a hint of recognition. His replies to your questions leave you with that leaning-on-the-edge-of-your-chair kind of anticipation, hoping that perhaps he'll say something more. He gives you the impression that he would neither harm you nor bring you unspeakable joy. Then again, he might be a good movie buddy, handyman, networking contact, or perhaps even a good boyfriend for one of your girlfriends.

Bachelor #3 is suave. He's smooth. Wasn't he on the cover of *GQ* last month? No, maybe it was *Esquire* or *Forbes*. Before you even begin to interview Bachelor #3, you can hear a third of the women in the audience screaming, "Number 3, Number 3, Number 3!"

If you were tempted to settle for imaginary Bachelor #1, #2, or #3 then your standards are too low. Every time you settle for a frog you shut the door on an opportunity to have your prince. You cheat yourself. Hold out for Bachelor #4, whose face will look incredibly familiar because you've imagined him so many times in your heart's eye. Wait until your heart flutters and you are breathless. Wait until you find a man who answers your questions with such natural ease that you think he might be telepathic. Wait until something inside of you just knows *it's him* and you want to run to him in slow motion but you know that would look entirely too tacky in public.

What "Better" Looks Like

By now, after reading six prince profiles, you should have a pretty decent picture of criteria to look for in a prince candidate. This shopping list from the women I interviewed should also come in handy.

❑ Good sense of humor	❑ Positive attitude
❑ Character and integrity	❑ Emotionally supportive
❑ Genuinely kind	❑ Monogamous
❑ Good communicator	❑ Honest
❑ Physically fit	❑ Respectful
❑ Romantic	❑ Supportive of my dreams
❑ Drug and alcohol free	❑ Supportive of my hobbies
❑ Has a job and makes enough to live comfortably	❑ Punctual and reliable
❑ Takes good care of himself	❑ Takes care of his children from other relationships

If you think the above list sounds about as boring as watching your future beloved file down a bunion, then you should know that you can still have punch, passion, fun and intrigue while you're having your practical love needs satisfied. Being practical doesn't have to be boooring. Feel free to add or delete items from the shopping list at your discretion. It's just a general checklist to steer you in a healthy direction. For instance, here are ten things 31-year-old recovering Frog Princess Heather added to her standards list after getting input from her adventurous, happily married best friend:

❑ Just looking at him gets me sexually aroused.
❑ He must be able to put together a romantic candlelit dinner or a picnic lunch.
❑ He must be spontaneous enough to pick me up from work,

blindfold me in the car, and whisk me off for an evening of fun.

❏ I want him spiritually rooted, but not such a fanatical stick in the mud that he wouldn't get dressed up as a ghoul for Halloween.

❏ I want him to dress well and comb his hair, and every now and then make a daring fashion statement.

❏ I want him to do the dishes and other housework and recycle without being asked, and maybe even turn up the music and dance in the middle of it all.

❏ I want him to come up with some creative apologies and make-up activities when he's wrong.

❏ He must have great stories to tell.

❏ He has to be nice to my children not only to make points with me, but because he thinks they're cool.

❏ If my mother was bearing down on me about my new hairstyle being too short, he would diplomatically escort her to the kitchen and ask her to knock it off.

A word to the wise: Coming up with your New Prince Standards list, which you'll be doing in a few minutes, is not a frivolous pursuit. Chew on it, sleep on it, revise and rewrite. On the other hand, it shouldn't be like writing your last will and testament either. Creating a mental picture of your prince-to-be can be one of the most enjoyable parts of ending your frog addiction.

Now it's your turn. Choose any of the preceding criteria or snatch them from deep inside your own heart, and write them down in your R & R Journal. Label that page My New Prince Standards List, Version 1. Keep reworking the list day after day until it represents the highest truth about what you really want in a man. The following questions may help you determine if you are finished.

1. What healthy things have I had in past men that I've really enjoyed?
2. What healthy things in past men have I not had that I wanted?
3. What things have I seen in another friend's man that I admire?
4. What things would I need to make the *whole* me happy?
5. Is there anything else?

   Hint: You should not have anything on your list that disqualifies every man on the planet, like a guy with one green eye and one blue one. Scrutinize each item.

Now guess what? You have to become everything on that list (if you're not already) so it's a fair exchange. How will you do that? When will you do it? Who will help you? Where will you need to go for self-improvement tools? Create a plan to help you make each item on your new standards list true in your own life.

Knowing You Deserve Better Than You've Had

If you've been scraping the bottom of the barrel for your dates or settling for less, there is a part of you that doesn't believe you deserve anything better, and if you don't think you're worthy of a prince, how will you get one? "My self-esteem bottomed out somewhere in my late teens," says 25-year-old Olivia. "I thought I was too tubby and plain to have cream-of-the-crop boyfriends, so I dated any guy who asked and often ended up regretting it."

Like Olivia, women with low self-regard are frog magnets. If you poison your mind with negative thoughts about yourself it will stunt your frog recovery, so work on changing your perception. Start by taking some time every day to stand in front of the mirror and recite affirmations that boost your self-image, like "I am divine," "I am willing to let go of all negative thoughts about myself," and "I deserve a prince." Remember, princes like women who like themselves. As a princely male friend once said, "I love a woman with confidence who acts like she likes herself. That makes her *very* attractive to me whether she looks like a glamour girl or not because she knows how to have fun packaging what she has."

Self-worth Lessons from Preschool

Thirty-one-year-old Charlie used to hate her hair and her freckles, until she borrowed a simple self-esteem exercise her 4-year-old freckled niece learned in preschool. Here's how it goes: Point to parts of your body from top to bottom and affirm positive statements. For example, "I like my hair, I like my eyes, I like my freckles, I like my lips . . . I like my hips . . . I like me."

Becoming a Connoisseur of Fine Things

Raising your self-esteem will help you feel better about yourself, which, believe it or not, is a thousand times more important than having a man. But it's only the beginning. Those feelings of joy and gratitude for who you are can overflow into your day-to-day activities, allowing you to cultivate discriminating tastes in whatever you do, from choosing the finest produce to the finest shampoo. Three people that I love from the center of my soul have taught me a lot about having the very best.

❧ My daughter, Esprit, who even as a toddler loved to hide underneath the nearest rack of expensive silk evening dresses in the department store while I was shopping. As a teenager, she shops for clothing with the same frou-frou precision that a top designer like Donna Karan might. If she gets home later and decides against a new piece after looking at it in the mirror from every possible angle and trying it on with the other items in her closet she bought it to complement, she will take it right back to the store for a refund.

❧ My honey Imhotep, who I've watched discriminatingly pick through a bin of cherries, apricots or grapes like he's choosing fruit for a king (which he is). In two years I've yet to see him buy one piece of unripe, or even minutely flawed piece of fruit. And to top it all off, if the fruit in the bins out front aren't up to snuff, he will ask the produce manager if he can see what's left in the back, or for the date of the next shipment.

❧ My best girlfriend Alma, who lives with all the flair and finesse of an empress, most recently applied her diva tastes to the remodeling of her home. After getting ideas from home design magazines and visiting the Street of Dreams—an annual event in Washington state where the public can tour about a dozen fancy "Lifestyles of the Rich and Famous" homes for a small fee—Alma sat down with her sketch pad and mapped out a new scheme for each room of her house, screened contractors and took bids, and refused to talk to anyone a second time who told her what she wanted could not be done.

Now, it's your turn. You can begin to grow better overall standards by first upping the flavor of your wardrobe, your culinary tastes and your home with these three fun exercises.

Exercise 1: A Trip to the Department Store

Go to your closet and put on one item that you love that needs a complementary piece. It could be the skirt or pair of pants that you wear with a so-so blouse that you settled for at the time because you were tired or frustrated with the search. Now, go to three department stores or boutiques where you often find clothes you enjoy. Try to find the perfect match. Then wear your new outfit immediately. Note: The same applies if you are looking for a pair of pants, a dress, shoes, a purse, or a neck scarf.

Exercise 2: A Trip to the Grocery Store or Restaurant

Think of your favorite meal and create a shopping list of the items you will need to prepare it. Go to the grocery store, the meat market, the bakery, the winery, or wherever else you need to go to get the supplies on your list. Whatever you buy, make sure you choose the very best, with all the care in the world. When you get back home, set the table with your best plates and candles, put on music you love and then prepare your feast.

If you'd rather go out for a delicious dinner or dessert at your favorite restaurant, spend at least fifteen minutes looking over the menu when you arrive. Then order your meal with sheer delight, specifying how you want it cooked and whether or not you want your sauces to the side or extra condiments. If there's a particular ingredient you don't want in it, ask to have it left out. If anything is not just the way you ordered it, send it back and wait for a suitable replacement. While you are eating, savor every bite.

Exercise 3: A Trip to the Home Accessories Store

Walk around your home and find something that's almost worn out, or unsuitable to your current tastes. It could be a shower curtain or a sofa, a teapot or a television. Imagine the item you would like standing in its place and stop at a few of your favorite places until you find what you're looking for. If it's a large item, have it delivered. If not, let one of the store personnel cart it out for you and load it into your vehicle. When you have it in your home, take time to stop and admire it every day, and point it out to guests when they enter your home.

What You Don't Know About Selecting Your Prince That Your Friends Might

I know, I know, you're grown. You can make your own decisions. Who wants their friends and family digging around in their love life anyway? Like it or not, they've already had a front seat with your love stories so far, so why not finally give them an open invitation to pitch you some constructive ideas about your future Mr. Right? One caveat: Do not solicit any advice from Frog Princesses.

Now, after you finish reading this step, I want you to go to the phone and call three of your friends or family members and ask them the questions below. While they are answering, I don't want you to interrupt, argue with them, accuse them of being crazy or hang up on them. I want you to listen and ingest everything they're saying as if it is a sacred blessing. And when they're finished I want you to genuinely thank them, meditate on what they've said, and update your prince standards list with any items that resonated with you. Here are the questions:

1. What type of man do you see me being happy and settled with?
2. What needs do you know I have that must be met to feel
   fulfilled in a relationship?
3. Has anyone ever met these needs for me? How?
4. What things have you liked about my former lovers/
   boyfriends/husband?
5. What things have you hated about my former lovers/
   boyfriends/husband?
6. What do you think I could do to attract a better quality
   man?
7. You'd do the jitterbug at my wedding if I was marrying whom?
8. What are my relationship weaknesses? My strengths?

Your Children May Have a Few Dating Pearls for You Too

When Esprit was about five or six, she used to be able to
predict when it would be sunny, and since we live in the rainy
state of Washington, this was always a long shot. She also
knew when I was bringing home take-out, where I hid her birthday presents, who I was talking to on the phone. Come to think
of it, it was very hard to surprise her, period. Her psychic radar
was about 90 percent accurate on my dates too. Because she
is a master at calibration, her innocent observations covered
the other 10 percent. "He doesn't feel right, Mom," she'd say.
"He doesn't listen when you talk to him." "He gives me the evil
eye when you aren't looking." "I saw a beer bottle in his trunk
when he put our skates in." And sometimes, frankly, when I
thought she was just being juvenile and mean-spirited, there

was some truth to her comments. She still refers to one man I dated years ago as "the one with the really big eyes who made us the meal without vegetables." He couldn't help the eye thing, but he could help that he already had a girlfriend when we started going out. Then there was the short one, the one who lived too far away and talked too fast, the one who hardly talked and the bossy one who looked like a football player.

Listen to what your children have to say about the new men in your life. Some of it might be acting out, but honor their insights. After all, your mating decisions will significantly affect their lives as well.

Having Two Sets of Standards

Suzette, 34, a publicist, confessed that she had two sets of standards for men: those for men she wanted to marry, and those for men she wanted to have sex with. "I know my marrying standards are too high for most men, but why should I have to strap on a chastity belt whenever I'm sexually attracted to a guy who doesn't quite suit my social and class norms? Like the last guy I bedded. His hair was a little greasy, he dressed like a thug and when he opened his mouth he sounded like one of the guys in *Dumb and Dumber*. I'd never be seen in public with him, but he washed up nicely and the sex was great."

This thought pattern goes under the category of massive brainwash and denial. Yes, sex is good, but ladies, if you're looking for a prince, then look for him. Stop making booty-call pit stops. They will only distract you and reverse all of the work you are doing to raise your standards. There are many ways to manage your lust, which I'll tell you about later.

Ask for What You Want; Work Out the Difference in Your Head

So now you have a new set of standards for choosing the next man in your life. Does that mean you'll get a prince who's a line-by-line match? Maybe yes, but probably no. Remarkably, my honey stepped off the pages of my standards list, unaltered. Ask for the best of the best when it comes to men. But if you've got ninety-nine items on your list and he's a couple short, work out the difference in your head.

Recovery Exercises

1. Wear or carry one of the items you bought in your clothing shopping spree exercise as often as you'd like for the next few weeks. Notice how having it on makes you feel and how others respond to it.
2. Make a list of three other areas of your life where you've been settling for less.

R & R Journal exercise: Circle all of the things on your New Prince Standards list that are non-negotiable.

Prince Dexter

Dexter, 36, is a native of Trinidad and Tobago and software engineer. His wife, 36-year-old Sabine, a native of Austria and culinary artist, shares their love story.

When I met Dexter, I didn't have any idea he was my prince. In fact, I did not like him very much at all. I was managing a bakery in Canada and he was always my "last minute" Saturday customer. Not only did he show up minutes before closing, but then he wanted to chat. I just wanted to close the store and go home to rest. I guess I was not showing my best manners.

But he was persistent in a gentlemanly way, and on our first date six months later, when he opened the car door for me, I was very impressed, so he got one bonus point for that. After my Bad Boy ex-husband I did not think that men with manners like his still existed.

Dexter and I fell in love immediately and discovered that we were true soul mates. We didn't have much in the material world when we first started out. He was a graduate student and I was working at the bakery, but we had each other, and that was all we needed.

We decided to get married about four months after that first date and we were on cloud nine. Shortly after, I became pregnant and I thought it could not get any better for us, but then we miscarried and our grief was enormous. Still, Dexter was right there for me all the time and we grew even closer together in our pain. He helped me to learn to laugh over and over again, as we suffered multiple miscarriages. Then finally our dream came true and we held our beautiful daughter in our arms. Tragically, our innocent happiness was shattered by the awful truth that our baby was very ill with a heart condition, and when she died nine months later, we were both broken and destroyed. Dexter was the most loving father I know and he would have done anything to save "his girl." Nevertheless, while he was grieving, he did everything to keep us sane and to help me when I did not want to move on anymore.

He's gotten so many bonus points in our six years of marriage that I've stopped counting them. I want to call him "King Dexter," for his unconditional love, honesty, support, care and his neverending strength.

STEP 8

Slow Down, Pay Attention

Lesson: Hottie or not, every man you meet is not a potential boyfriend, lover or partner. If you learn to objectively explore his possibilities and pitfalls before jumping into a relationship, you'll lower your chances of winding up in frog canyon.

Affirmations

1. I like to take my time choosing partners and friends.
2. A date is just a date.
3. I take the time to do my date warm-ups and review my standards list before each date.

How many times, after a brief episode of ogling, flirting, or hearing your fix-up coordinator run down the stats on a new man have you decided he was your soul mate? And how many times were you painfully, even morbidly, mistaken?

Healthy, practical love choices take time, careful observation, consideration and educated assessments. If you don't want another frog in your midst you're going to have to slow down and pay attention long enough to see if being with a new man really makes sense in your life.

A Date Is Just a Date

When I asked some single women recently for their definition of "date," I got a wide range of fascinating answers:

- 🐸 It's a chance to get a free meal and entertainment.
- 🐸 It's what you do before you have sex.
- 🐸 It's something I have to keep doing until I find Mr. Right.
- 🐸 It's what you need to do so people don't think you're weird.
- 🐸 It's a prelude to marriage or a long-term relationship.
- 🐸 It's what my mom hopes I'll do again one day.
- 🐸 It's a chance to go out and have fun and companionship with someone.

It can be all of these things and more, but at its best a date is simply a prime, non-contractual opportunity to get to know a man better. Nothing has to follow a date. Not a kiss, not a second date, not a long-term relationship. Looking at it this way will keep you more grounded, mindful and in control of any negative triggers and relationship fantasies that may have sent you stumbling down froggy lane in the past.

Someone once said that we often look without seeing, listen without hearing, and eat without tasting. Dating is no exception. How many times have you sealed a first date without any conscious regard for the man you've just spent two or three hours with? Were you too busy trying to figure out how he would look in the light of the crystal touch lamp next to your bed or what his credit card limit was to gauge his attention span and communication skills? How clearly do you recall the way he greeted you, bid you farewell, or anything in between? The more time you take, the more attention you pay, the more your odds of choosing a prince will increase.

First-Date Warm-ups

Of course it would be easier to say that a date is just a date if your pet collie hadn't beaten you hands down in the love department for the last few months, or if the guy you were getting ready to go out with didn't make you want to scream out, "Hallelujah, he has come!" Not to worry though, these date warm-ups will help you stabilize yourself:

1. *Date in daylight.* Arrange a museum date, or a hike, or something else that says "hey I think I like you and I'm trying to get to see if I really like you enough to have a second date which might or might not lead to another date." Remember, you want to be able to study him and that is much easier to do while trekking up a quiet, sunlit mountain trail than in a noisy, smoke-filled disco. The additional good news: Many frogs have just as much of an aversion to daylight as vampires, so you'll be able to eliminate them more quickly when you see them melting down before you.

2. *Review your New Prince Standards list* prior to your date for a quick, centering refresher of what's important to you in a male companion.

3. *Decide beforehand* in an innocent, adventurous way

that you're going to pretend to be a historian or a private eye and piece together his story while you're on the date.

4. *Do not overdress or overprepare for a date.* No need to open the door looking like a hobo, but if you want to see a man's true nature in a relatively short period of time, show him yours. Take off the Wonderbra and the high heels, slip into a comfortable outfit that's already in your closet, go easy on the makeup, and lose the hair spray.

5. *Bury your expectations.* If he shines, fine, go out on another date. If he doesn't, you still have you.

Slowing Yourself Down Even More

After replaying her date until 5 A.M. the next morning, 27-year-old Rondie, a chemist, wrote his name after hers over a hundred times, and genetically surmised that their children would be brunette like her. In human time, she had spent four hours with him, but in her mind it was like four dog years. And yet, she did not realize until three months into their relationship that not five minutes into their first date he had mentioned that he was in counseling for depression. Therese, 31, on the other hand, went to a semi-romantic movie on her first date with frog Rick, and although they'd barely said two words to each other the whole time other than "Excuse me" and "Do you want more popcorn?" she says, "I found myself wondering if he would take studio portraits with me to send to my family for the holidays. It wasn't until a month later on another movie date that I noticed him getting excited when a woman got beat up. Why was I shocked the first time he slapped me?"

We've all been there, or close, or we know someone who has. We get so excited and enchanted by a man's physical presence or our picture-perfect possibilities that we fail to conduct objective inspection and research or tune in to the little intuitive shepherd in our head who butts in to our dreamy thoughts with, "Uh-unh. He's not for you, girl." Every time you go out on a date with an individual you should have your imaginary Standards list superimposed on his chest, and you should be checking it off as the evening goes on, by engaging all of your senses.

1. *See.* Pretend you are a newly sighted person discovering him for the first time, perform a nonchalant head-to-toe survey of his face, his neck, his chest, his arms, and so on down to his feet. If he has a mole on his left cheek, when you close your eyes and think about him later you should see it in your mind's eye.

2. *Listen* to what he's really saying, not just what you want to hear. Note the tone of his voice. Is it warm and inviting, sincere, kind, or enthusiastic? Or is it harsh to the ear, too fast, dull or rehearsed?

3. *Touch* him on the hand or shoulder while you're talking to him, and see if he's jerky or receptive to non-sexual human contact. If he touches you, is his touch light? Watch how he touches other things too, like doors (if he opens them). How does he handle his food and utensils? What's the weight of his step? If he kisses you goodnight, or shakes your hand, is it tender or rough?

4. *Taste.* Well, you are probably not going to be tasting him on the first date, but if you do get a quick kiss, what's going on inside of his mouth? Does he taste salty or sweet? Like onions or garlic or honey and cinnamon? Smokey or pure?

5. *Smell.* Is he wearing a hint of Old Spice or musk body oil? Does he smell Zestfully clean or muy musty? Does he have a refreshing manly scent, or remind you of baby powder?

People tell you a lot about themselves, every moment—good and bad. The more you rev up your senses, the more clues you will get about them, and you'll pay more attention to others in the future. Here are a few examples of what your inner dialogue could sound like on a date when you employ your five senses:

Carina's Date with Rocky

When he leaned in to hug me (and why was he hugging me on a first date?) he smelled like fish. Not fish he'd just eaten either, but like he'd just gotten off a fishing boat in Alaska. Nice eyes, though. Clear blue. They remind me of the waters of Tahiti. But why was he talking so loud? It was totally annoying. Like he was a sports announcer or something. And I was sitting right next to him. I didn't want to kiss him because I knew I'd taste dead fish in his mouth.

Lucy's Date with Marco

His voice was so tranquil that I quickly forgot I'd had such a nutty day at work. Great manners too. I can't remember the last time a man held out a chair for me. He tipped the waitress well too. I have this picture of him being the kid who cleaned the teacher's erasers in kindergarten, just because he wanted to help out. And his goodbye kiss was gentle, and if I'm not mistaken, he sighed afterwards.

Bonnie's Date with Jonathan

We met at the mall and he tried to take over the whole date. Bossy, bossy, bossy. When I suggested we go and look at CDs, he grabbed my arm and pulled me into the video arcade without so much as an apology for the finger marks on my arm. He could stand to lose that five o'clock shadow too.

Use Your Sixth Sense, Your Intuition

If any impressions come up about your date that don't fit any of the five senses, they are probably intuitive footnotes. Treat them with the same reverence you give the other data you collect instead of discarding them as woo-woo *Twilight Zone* script starters. Naomi, 21, went out with a guy who answered her personal ad, and even though she couldn't quite figure out why she had an eerie feeling about him, she didn't let him into her apartment when he walked her to the door, and she never went out with him again. About a year later she found out he'd been arrested for rape a few days after their date. Twenty-nine-year-old Melody went out with a respected lawyer, but over dinner she felt unpleasant emotions coming up for no reason that reminded her of her alcoholic ex. It turns out he checked into a rehab center later that year for cocaine abuse.

Slowing Your Date Down

We're not the only ones rushing romance. Men sometimes have rushy-rush early relationship agendas too. Have any of these things ever happened to you after a first or second date?

❧ He tries to take privileges with you that really require much more familiarity.

❧ He said he was glad he could cancel his personal ad.

❧ You go out on one little so-so date with a co-worker and the next day he brags you're his girlfriend.

❧ He wanted to know if you had an extra toothbrush in the middle of dinner.

❧ He asked what size ring you wore before he knew your middle name.

How about these rushy-rush men:

❧ "I took my boyfriend home for Christmas to meet my family after two months of dating, and he proposed to me over the family toast."

❧ "After lunch with a new co-worker, he e-mailed to thank me, and then again later in the day to wish me a safe ride home and a pleasant evening. In the morning, there were three more e-mails from him before nine. "Are you okay?" "What size skis do you wear?" "Want to have lunch?"

❧ "One morning as I was getting dressed, I heard the guy I'd just started dating call in to a radio station and ask one of the hosts if it was too early to tell the girl he'd been seeing for ten days (me) that he was falling in love with her. The host challenged him to express himself, and as if I wasn't sure it was him already, my phone started to ring."

How to Slow Your Dates Down

1. *Clarify your new dating philosophy with him in advance.* It will take you approximately ten seconds to say the following: "Let's take it one date at a time, enjoy ourselves and if we both agree at the end of the date to continue we will." If he's got prince potential, he may actually breathe a sigh of relief because he didn't have to say it first.

2. *Skip the sex.* I know, I know. It's a new millennium. Doesn't he expect you to have sex with him? And don't you want to? Don't get me wrong. Sex is good, with the right person, at the right time. However, premature sex with a questionable man can be disastrous. Why? If you are like most women, sex equals the end of *objectivity*, the end of a grounded "discovery" period with the new guy, the end of a casual relationship and often the beginning of I-L-O-V-E-Y-O-U. What's the fix? Keep your at-the-front-door date goodbyes short, sweet and virtuous. Also, drop a few ice cubes down your blouse when you get inside.

3. *Shooing and fleeing* work very well too if you never want to see him again. I mean, what is there after that, except to go into repel mode. (See Step 6.) However, if you'd like to see him again and think he's made innocent testosterone boo-boos, then do one and two.

Slowing Your Friends and Family Down

Okay, so you've put the brakes on yourself and your date. What about Aunt Nan and your best girl who often get more excited than you over a new prospect? Twenty-three-year-old April's aunt wanted to invite a guy April had gone out with once on the family camping trip. "When I said I didn't think that was appropriate she asked, 'Well, is he gay?' "

And what about your incorrigible—but well-meaning—friends? "My friends go overboard more than I do sometimes," admitted 34-year-old Deanne. "They get their hopes up over a cracker crumb, and that sets off a chain reaction and pretty soon there's a whole cast of people who become an audience for my love life. One time I casually mentioned to my friend Cinnie in an e-mail that I saw a cute guy at the latte stand outside my office. And guess what? She forwarded that e-mail to five other co-workers, who snooped around the surrounding office buildings like bloodhounds until they located him. An hour later, one of them e-mailed me his name, office number, birthplace, birthdate and license plate number—which his receptionist surrendered in the name of sister solidarity—and wanted to know when I was going to pop by and invite him out."

Tips for Slowing Down Your Friends

1. *Don't tell.* Keep your longings and lustings for strangers, co-workers and neighbors to yourself. If you don't draw early-bird attention to your dates, you won't be picked at by your friends for updates. If you *must* tell someone, try "Dear Diary."

2. *Play your dates down.* If your friends or family set you up, and they insist on after-date briefings, whether you're in like or not, pretend you aren't. And you will have to be good at this, because if they detect even the tiniest stifled sigh they'll pry until you crack. If you can, answer inquisitions over the phone so they won't be able to read

your face. Here's what you do: Answer their questions with the least words possible: "yes," "no," "maybe," "okay" and "I don't know yet" will get you through most of the interrogations.

3. *Give yourself a 24-hour no-contact cooling off period.* After a sweet date, a lot of women pick up the phone and call their best girlfriends to share the afterglow. Don't. Most of us who've been in deep like half a dozen times know that most of this was trumped-up, gooey-girl hype a few months down the road when he's fallen out of our good graces. Give yourself time to float back down to Earth so you can follow the guidelines in number two.

Note: If he does turn out to be a significant part of your life, then graciously take the heat from the people you kept out of the loop.

One Date at a Time

The preceding tips will help you get through the first level of screening. If after that, you have any notion whatsoever that you are dating a frog, the experiment has failed. Abort.

However, if he passes the first level of screening, evaluate each subsequent date on the same scale each time you go out with him or talk to him on the phone. You should be enjoying his company, but you should also be grading him on at least one item on your New Prince Standards list. This is how you will reveal the Frog Type II that I mentioned in the previous step. Be alert.

Standards	date 1	date 2	date 3	date 4
Good communication skills				

Along with post-date report cards, if you decide to continue dating a particular man, it wouldn't hurt to run the following battery of questions on yourself:

1. Do I enjoy his company and have positive thoughts about seeing him?
2. Do any big "if onlys" come to mind when I think of him?
3. What's different about this relationship from others I've had?
4. What would I be most afraid to see in this man?
5. Am I still grounded enough to walk away from him if I do see it?

Internet Dates Don't Count

The techniques I've provided you with so far work in person. I don't think you can conduct a proper screening and investigation over the Internet. Men hiding behind a keyboard can lie or exaggerate, and they also tend to have very poor social skills, but you knew that, right?

Anonymity and mystery are often intriguing, but for all you know, you could be finger dating with the next Son of Sam, a prisoner in Club Fed, or some little pimply pubescent 13-year-old boy.

"I met a guy over the Internet once who turned out to be a freak of nature in every way. We met at a coffee shop after three months of e-dating. He never looked at me the whole two hours. Then the next night he e-mailed to say he was so struck by my beauty that it rendered him speechless, and sent me a Robert Frost poem. I went out with him a second time and same thing. It was as if he had a keyboard personality and an in-person one. And I didn't like the in-person version at all," sighed Amber, 38.

"Me too," says 25-year-old Sarah. "I went out with a man I met online and all he could do was talk about how great my letters were. He even brought copies of them along to discuss over dinner. I thought we were going to take our relationship to the next level, but he wanted me virtually."

Thirty-year-old Gloria's date wasn't painfully shy or obsessed with her letters, but he wasn't buff either, like he had bragged in his personal ad. "When he showed up at the restaurant I looked up at his pregnant belly and almost gagged. What part of 'buff' had he not understood?"

You will save yourself a lot of time if you conduct your screenings in person and if the two of you are living in the same state so you have time to see him often, in a variety of different situations.

Recovery Exercises

1. Practice saying "I'm going to take my love life one date at a time."
2. Recall at least one significant thing you saw, heard, touched, tasted, or smelled on your last date.

R & R Journal exercise: Create a list of places you can go on a date during the day.

Prince Jared

Three years ago when 40-year-old Jasmine found out she had breast cancer, her husband of twelve years took a leave of absence from his job to take her to doctor's appointments, research the disease, look into alternative medicines, and work toward a cure.

When I first found out, I was so depressed and sullen that I didn't even have the notion to fight, but Jared had enough fight and hope for both of us. Finding a cure for me became his full-time job, and if he wasn't rubbing my toes or fixing me one of the weird herbal concoctions some healer said to try, he was on the computer searching for something else that would stop my cancer from spreading. At the end of each day, he'd gather up all of his papers and we'd huddle in the den with his latest findings. He's always had a coach-like personality, so he delivered each one in his native rah-rah spirit. Because of him, I tried so many things that were new to me—herbs, acupuncture, visualization, vitamins. None of them stopped the cancer from spreading, but my overall health improved, which I can imagine made me more resistant in the end.

We opted for chemotherapy after several months of alternative treatments because the cancer was trying to take over the rest of my body. I say "we" because I truly believe he felt everything I felt—the nausea, the disorientation, the pain, the rage, the despair.

But he never gave up, not even when I gave up after the mastectomy, which still did not make me cancer free. I started telling him that I was going to die and I wanted him to be happy and love again. I wanted him to have children and build his dream house with my replacement. But each time I tried to let go of my life, he tried to give it back to me. The day I insisted on overhauling my will, he planted a tree in the backyard. When I asked him to take me to Paris again so I could see it one last time, he winked at me and said we'd go back on my 50th birthday and took me to Disney World instead. We rode on everything— even the kiddie rides—for hours until I was bursting with laughter. When I tried to give away my baby clothes, which I'd been saving for our first born, he salvaged them from the give-away box and had them made into a quilt that still hangs on the ceiling above our bed. When I went into remission, he started to cry, for the very first time since our ordeal began, and got down on one knee and asked me to marry him again, after he recited our favorite line from our favorite children's movie, *Mulan:* "It is a rare flower that blooms in adversity."

STEP 9

See It Through

Lesson: If you are going to have a healthier love life, you are going to need the courage, backbone and the faith to see it through. That means learning to fortify yourself against periods of lust, desperation and fear, and keeping the faith, no matter what.

Affirmations

1. I finish what I start and I keep the faith.
2. I will keep my heart open to love even when it fails.
3. Fulfilling my own sexual desires pleases me.

Now for the million-dollar questions: Do you believe having a prince is worth the effort? And if he doesn't show up tomorrow, or next month, or next year, will you still believe? Do you think you'll grow weary of gagging your former Frog Princess self whenever she starts to spew out reckless frog propaganda, like "I know he's got a girlfriend, but he only asked me to a matinee." What if your last low-life ex sneaks up on you at the park at a weak moment and whispers in your ear, "You're all I think about, all I love. Please give me another chance?" and when you speed-dial your frog recovery sponsor on your cell phone her line is busy? How are you going to stand up for yourself and honor your decision to choose healthy relationships twenty-four, seven, three-sixty-five?

What the Eye Doesn't See, the Heart Doesn't Yearn For

This old common-sense Chinese proverb should nip most of your froggy cravings in the bud in your battle of the backbone. Simply put, if you think you won't be able to resist froggy temptations, do not go where they are, and do not invite them to be where you are. If you are still going to your favorite frog metropolises out of habit, and fighting off one frog after another, then find new haunts. Twenty-five-year-old Brenda moved her Friday TGIF celebration with her co-workers from a nearby bar to a Thai restaurant with a karaoke machine instead. "I liked hanging out with them after a whirlwind work week, but when we got to the bar, I spent 90 percent of my time chasing off frogs. The cuter they got, the more pitiful my 'go-away' orders became. Now we go to the restaurant, order gobs of food to share and see who can get the most laughs at karaoke."

Twenty-nine-year-old Terri says, "I used to invite my ex over for Christmas dinner because he was still my brother's best friend, but this year I didn't and it was such a relief not to have him corner me in the kitchen and have to put up with his begging, whining let's-get-back-together stuff."

One day you will probably have to stand in the center of one of your favorite places, with your willpower alone shielding you from an invasion of a frog army (try a day at the beach in July), but why open yourself up to others that you could easily avoid by exercising your creative distancing options?

If necessary, dump old friends who are counteractive. Just because you're on the road to relationship riches doesn't mean everyone you know is going to pack a sack lunch and join you. Thirty-year-old Tamara, a recovered Frog Princess, quit accepting social invitations from her sorority sister who still had a hearty frog appetite. "The day I had to hail a cab after a basketball game because she went chasing after one of the players during intermission and never returned to her seat, or answered my pages, was the last time I went anywhere with her."

Look around your home. Have you gotten rid of pictures, mementos, and other reminders of frogs past? Are you all stocked with pampering supplies and enough hobbies and passions to keep your mind and hands occupied? Are you at peace? Are you on a mission? Do you schedule fun "dates" with your family and friends? Are you living juicy? (See Step 4.) Whether you're on the beach or at a restaurant, plan to have fun wherever you go, without froggy interference, and you will.

The Secret to 24-7 Backbone

Integrity can either be a killjoy or your most powerful willpower tool. Who really wants to be a noble, Goody Two-shoes all the time? Why can't the empowered you and naughty you have equal time? I remember an angelic, empowered woman friend who was going through a hard time after her divorce asking me, "When do I get to be a bitch?" In that instance she wanted permission to be weak, to stop working so diligently to get along with her troublesome, nitwit ex-husband for her daughter's sake, to be something other than the glorious light she has been all these years. "Is that what you really want?" I asked. And a few moments later, through tears and laughter, she said, "No. Forget I said that, okay?"

That's integrity. It's forgoing the urge to do something weak (and possibly evil) so you can have a momentary thrill, and choosing instead to take the high road and be true to your principles. Here's how to keep your integrity up so you can have healthier romantic relationships permanently:

❧ *Put your soul to it.* Willpower and backbone are not something you can just pull out of your pocket in the middle of a passion flash. You'll need to cultivate it beforehand by developing a spiritual practice. Begin by taking some time each day to meditate or to pray on the higher purpose of your life and to spend quiet time renewing your spirit. A lot of single women pray the prayer of desperation: "God, please send me a man, today." Try praying for the strength and the dignity to live a beautiful, enchanted, purposeful life, while also praying to be prepared for a man who wants to live that way too. Meditate on this question: "How can I discover what I really need to be happy with myself at this moment?"

❧ *Monitor your integrity meter* throughout the day. You must be able to be your own frog recovery sponsor by scanning yourself frequently so you'll know when you're about to go astray. Start by thinking about the last time you did something without integrity. Wasn't there some internal warning signal, like a weird feeling in the pit of your stomach, a wave of nausea, a headache or some other body tension, a silent or soft whisper of "don't do it, girl"? If you figure out what your internal warning signals are and learn to heed them, you'll be able to maintain your integrity more.

❧ ***Stand back and take a strategic look at the larger picture*** of what it would mean to forsake yourself. Will accepting a date with a frog lead to further froggy entanglement? What will going to a nightclub after you've just broken up with your boyfriend get you? Are you opting for instant gratification, or does this act really say that you are being true to your goal of finding a prince?

❧ ***Critical questioning.*** A little self-questioning can keep you on the straight and narrow. Sometimes, that moment when you have to pause to come up with an answer will be enough to break your state if you're running out the door to meet what's-his-name. Here are ten questions to start with:

1. Why am I doing this?
2. What would it take to give myself permission to do something else at this moment?
3. Is there too much drama here?
4. What do I really desire? Will my behavior lead to it?
5. What is my true intention?
6. What healthy thing will come out of this?
7. What unhealthy thing will come out of this?
8. How can I be strong right now?
9. How will I explain this to my frog recovery sponsor?
10. What happened the last time I did this?

❧ ***Ride the wave.*** You know you don't have to act on every temptation, right? Try holding on to a thought for a moment, really holding on to it with all of your might. Your mind wanders, doesn't it? I mean, unless you've got a mental death grip on a thought, it will pass in a few seconds. If you want to avoid breaching your no-more-frogs vow, practice riding the thought wave with negative temptations that come up on your road to prince until they pass through your mind. For instance, the next time you're feeling your backbone slipping, note what's going on in your head—all of it—without any emotion or promises, prior to actually acting on it. Your inner script might sound something like this, "Hmmm . . . I notice I really have a temptation to call what's-his-name. I'm feeling a little horny, a little blue . . . Wow, it's raining outside. What's his number again, anyway? I really shouldn't do it . . . but it would be fun to see him . . . I wonder if I have any popcorn? . . ." After a while, you'll notice your thoughts of sabotage floating off into the atmosphere like balloons.

❧ *Learn to correct your course quickly.* If you feel your integrity slipping off center, bravely rework your behavior until you're back on course. This can include calling up a frog you've accepted a date with and saying, "I'm sorry, I won't be able to go out with you after all. I made a rash decision and I know now that it was a mistake because you *(fill in the blank)* and I *(fill in the blank)*."

The more you practice honoring your decision to make better choices about how you spend your love, the better you'll become at it.

Here are some opportunities to practice getting back on course:

❧ When you feel yourself wanting to call an ex just to get your books back, books that you cannot even remember the titles of.

✢ When you take your old boyfriend's shirt out of the Goodwill box, just so you can wear it once more for old time's sake.

✢ When you call a psychic hotline to see if things are going to get any better with a guy you've already identified as a frog.

✢ When you're caught up in the holiday or wedding spirit and you think it would be okay to have one little mistletoe kiss with Frog X.

What About Sex?

A grown woman told me the other day that she thought she'd lose her touch if she didn't have sex again soon. I mean, really. Is she a Frog Princess waiting to happen or what? If you ever become a total klutz in the bedroom due to lack of sexual activity, *The National Enquirer* may want to do an article on you titled something like "Woman Abstinent for Months, Forgets How to Have Sex." Because I was celibate for three whole years, I can tell you with absolute certainty that you will not lose your touch. Sex is one of those things, like learning to ride a bike, that you never, ever forget. You may tuck it away for a few seasons, but the next time you take it out for a spin, your body will remember exactly what to do. You also won't dry up, burst or lose your desire either.

Simply put, sex is better with princes. You get a deliciously deep triple love-passion-sacred connection. You also avoid the unwanted complications of contracting a lifelong reminder of a foolish frog blooper—STDs or pregnancy. I wish that I could have won this argument with a woman I once served with in the army who we'll call Private Dean. Like me, she was in her twenties at the time and her claim to fame was that she was the battalion slut. She snuck out of our barracks every night for indiscriminate orgies over in the guys' barracks. After a month of lecturing, I offered to go running with her every time she had an orgy-like craving. I think it would have worked permanently if she'd have been in better shape, but, alas, she only took me up on it twice, and as she came panting around the corner where I waited for her the second time, she looked at me and said, "You're crazy, you know. Sex is more fun than running. I'll see you later." And she limped off to the guys' barracks. Unfortunately, numerous STDs later, she was still at it.

Lust Management

Sexual desire is healthy. You don't have to squash it. But careless lust can get you into the same trouble it got Private Dean into. The trick is to find a healthy sexual or sensual outlet that will not interfere with your new commitment to date and marry smart, or to learn to breathe through it the way women are taught to breathe through labor pains. She who can fulfill her own sexual desires rules, and she can also teach the next man in her life how to pleasure her. The next time you're having a hot, restless night, try these:

Six Passion Breaks for One

1. *Masturbate.* Yes, I said it. I really wanted to say self-pleasuring because it sounds more eloquent and divine, but in the past when I've asked women if they self-pleasure, they've stared at me blankly. "Masturbate," on the other hand, always gets a ready nod. Through masturbation you can discover every erotic zone on your body with your hand or a vibrator, but don't forgo household

appliances either. One girlfriend told me that she climaxes in less than two minutes with the "under the faucet" or "shower head" technique by letting the trickle of water land repeatedly on her clitoris. Experiment, read, and be willing to really enjoy touching yourself and become more comfortable with your body. The bonus is, the better you know your own body and feel comfortable with it, the easier it will be to illustrate to your man. You can pick up a vibrator at some drugstores, most adult toy shops and Good Vibrations (1-800-289-8423), a company owned by women that has been helping women explore their sexuality since 1977, which offers a great mail-order catalog.

2. *Learn to be more sensual in non-sexual ways.* Try this simple exercise right now if you're in a private place. Trace your lips with your finger and then put it into your mouth and seductively lick and suck it. One woman I know finds eating foods like strawberries with whipped cream, or bananas extremely titillating. Another massages her body with luscious scented oil by candlelight.

3. *Indulge in virtual sex with a hot fantasy partner.* Make up a feature-perfect amorous imaginary lover who turns you on in every way, or fly in an imaginary version of your favorite celebrity crush and imagine him fulfilling your biggest sexual fantasy, over and over again.

4. *Watch a sexually explicit movie.* One woman said, "The way I learned what to do sexually was by watching a porno movie once and noting the way the other women touched themselves." If you want something tastefully erotic with a nice plot, rent *Kama Sutra*, which is based on an ancient Indian lovemaking guide of the same name. If you want something sweaty and X-rated,

you'll have plenty to pick from at the video sections of most adult entertainment stores. Don a wig, dark glasses and a trench coat if you're too embarrassed to be seen or request a mail order catalog from Good Vibrations. They have a library of adult videos.

5. *Take up a sexy hobby.* Belly dancing and body painting are two good places to start, or with anything else that makes you feel *all woman.* "Feeling sexy is very important to me," says Winona, a 36-year-old department store clerk who takes tango lessons twice a week. "I cut back on eating out so I could have the budget for my lessons and outfits. The tango makes me feel alive and desirable!"

6. *Buy sexy lingerie* or clothing to adorn yourself. Wear the special lingerie to bed once a week, taking time to admire yourself before the mirror.

Sexual desire can also be satisfied in non-sexual ways too. During the celibate years of my frog recovery I dearly missed the afterglow following lovemaking, which made me feel special and loved. More than almost anything else, I longed for the silky, whispered sweet nothings, long appreciative glances, and spooning.

After some pouting and skulking one Valentine's Day when I was babysitting a friend's daughter so that she and her husband could enjoy a romantic evening out, I decided to compose a list of ways I could conjure up those same feelings without having sex. I came up with ten, which coincidentally partnered nicely with masturbation, watching sexy movies, and all of the passion breaks mentioned above. Pick one—or all—of these the next time you want to love yourself without a vibrator:

1. Read a book of love poems and pretend that each one was specially authored for you.
2. Give yourself a foot rub.
3. Call your home number and fill up your voice mail with compliments.
4. Cuddle with a plush, stuffed animal.
5. Take a candlelit bath.
6. Dedicate a song to yourself on the radio.
7. Hug yourself.
8. Send yourself an endearing friendship card.
9. Scent your pillows and sheets with perfume.
10. Tenderly kiss your hand.

Just in case none of the above ideas work, prepare an emergency kit, which includes at the bare minimum:

- *The number of your frog recovery sponsor.* Tape it to the phone if you have to. Call her if none of the above lust management ideas work for you and you are seriously considering getting some sexual healing of the froggy kind.
- *A pack of cards.* Playing solitaire one hundred times will squash even the most persistent sexual urge.
- *Chewing gum.* It will give you something to do with your mouth.
- *A good book.* Not a romance novel or magazine either. Try some self-help, finance, health, and foreign language tutorials.
- *A list of three to five three-hour-long household chores* like cleaning out the basement, painting the garage, or re-wallpapering your kitchen.

Managing Your Emotions During Recovery

Just as having healthy solitary sexual outlets can help you physically survive dry spells, having a healthy emotional rapport with yourself will also improve your odds of going the distance. I have seen many women sabotage their recoveries with negative thinking, which leads to emotional distress. For example, 27-year-old Allison was six months into a model frog recovery when she went back to her old frog boyfriend, Davis. "I felt myself weakening one day. I hadn't been on a date in a long, long time, and I was lonely and depressed. With each day, those feelings grew stronger, and after a while I decided Davis was better than waiting forever for the perfect guy." Raven, 32, also found her frog recovery pledge burdensome after a few weeks. "I wanted to have a man tell me I was pretty and sexy. It was all I could think about some days." Unlike Allison, however, Raven avoided a relapse by expressing her unhealthy cravings in her journal and complimenting herself. "Once I figured out that I could take care of my own emotional needs—tell myself I was pretty and sexy—I felt this overwhelming sense of power and commitment. Like I could hang on forever until I have a man who is worthy of me."

In addition to managing your emotions by journaling, try affirmations, meditation, prayer, and exercise.

Keep the Faith

A long time ago, I remember reading a story about a single mom who started medical school at age 42. She had her doubts and fears about whether she'd make it through since all of her classmates were almost half her age and she'd been out of school almost as long as they'd been alive. She also had her guilt about farming her two children out to her parents more nights than she could remember so she could study.

One particular night, she arrived at school an hour early for class to study, but instead of rushing in to meet her lab partner, she was overwhelmed with sadness about snapping at her son for not keeping up with his chores and she started to cry. When her tears were all gone, she thought about what it would be like to look down from the podium at her graduation and see him sitting next to his brother, and her parents and the friends and family who had cheered her on. And she thought about her future patients and how she could help them, and how wonderful it would feel to fulfill her dream, and then she wiped her face, grabbed her bookbag and ran in to meet her study partner, still half crying, half laughing. She also went on to graduate, with her sons and family beaming at her with pride and love.

Some days you will be overcome with fear, doubts, ambiguity, withdrawal symptoms and transitional discomfort. That's just the way it is when you are moving from here to there. *And it's okay.* Faith does not mean you will have a prevailing sense of righteousness about what you're doing every day, but it means that you will do what you think is right anyway. Willpower eventually turns into knowingness and you won't have to put as much effort into it. If you keep moving toward what you want, you will have it, but you and you alone will have to see it through.

Recovery Exercises

1. Think of a few ways you can distance yourself even more from frogs past (places you can stop going to, mutual friends you can avoid, etc.).
2. Put together a lust management kit using any of the techniques and tools above.

3. Practice checking your integrity meter tomorrow in each thing you do. Ask yourself if your actions support your new goals.

R & R Journal exercise: Make a list of positive things you've done in the past to recover from heartbreak and how you kept the faith that something better would come out of it.

Prince X

One dark, stormy night, I got my first flat tire at a well-lit mall and wondered why I hadn't taken shop in high school instead of home economics. When I stepped out of my car to survey the situation, a man came out of the mall and walked to his car, which was next to me. As I stood there, rain trickling down my face, I asked him stupid question number 1. "Do you think I could drive another ten minutes to my home on this flat?" "No way," he said, smiling. "Do you know how to fix it?" "Uh-unh," I said, waving my AAA card. "Do you have a jack and a spare?" he asked.

Proudly, I led him to my trunk, lifted the particleboard covering and pointed to the spare doughnut that I had discovered just last month after dropping my favorite bracelet while unloading groceries. "What about a jack?" he asked. Stupid question number 2: "Do those come with the car?"

He smiled the way I think he would have smiled at his sister, never making one audible dumb woman remark, and went to his car to fetch his rain gear, and then came back and retrieved a jack from underneath my particleboard. What do you know? It was like watching a magician pull scarves out of an empty hat. Then he stuck his hand back under the board and fished around for something he called a Universal wrench. When he came up empty, he said, "Mall security guards usually carry them," and marched into the mall to borrow one.

Back at my car minutes later, still dressed impeccably in crisp business slacks and a white shirt underneath his rain slicker, he slid off the old tire and slid on the new one, without so much as a dirt smudge on himself, telling me step-by-step what he was doing while I held the flashlight.

"Who taught you to do this?" I asked him. "My dad," he said. "He wouldn't give me the car keys until I learned to fix a flat. I've been trying to teach my daughter and my wife for years. Wouldn't want them getting stranded anywhere. It's funny, they're both what you would call twenty-first-century women, except when it comes to changing tires."

Then I knew that he had gone the extra step not just because he was a random do-gooder, but because he had a wife and a daughter, and probably a sister and other women he wanted to keep safe in the world, and for the moment, I reminded him of them.

After I thanked him, he waited for me to drive off before he left. I chuckled at the thought that he would undoubtedly sum his good deed up in the brief, oversimplified way men do when his wife asked where he'd been and why his shoes were soaked: "I changed a lady's flat at the mall."

Lesson: You don't need dating services or personal ads, singles bars or psychic hotlines to attract your prince. Every day, be the best you that you can be, and he will come.

Affirmations

1. As I create a rich, memorable life, I also create the synergy for my prince to appear.
2. I have the patience to wait for a love that's worth it.
3. When I do find my prince, I will keep things juicy.

One night, Tiffany was sobbing so long over not having a man in her life that her tears formed a puddle on the floor. Much to her surprise, within seconds, a kindly looking old woman appeared from the puddle and said, "Hush, girl, and bring me a beautiful flower, a movie ticket stub, and a doggie bag from that Italian restaurant you like and I will ease your troubles." Tiffany looked up hopefully and dried her eyes. The flower was easy. She went outside and plucked a beautiful rose from her garden and handed it to the old woman. Then she drove to the cinema and watched a comedy she'd been wanting to see but didn't want to attend alone. Then she went to her favorite Italian restaurant, her cheeks still flushed from laughing so hard at the movie, and requested a table for one. She ordered her meal, and took a sip of wine, thinking, "This going out alone isn't so bad after all." Just then the waiter appeared and interrupted her thoughts. He pointed to a handsome gentleman who wanted to know if he could join her. She nodded, and he slid into the booth opposite her, and they spent two delightful hours together. On parting, they decided to get together the following weekend for a game of tennis. Tiffany rushed home to tell the old woman about her good fortune and to give her the warm plate of lasagna and garlic bread. But the old woman was not there. There was just a note that read, "I hope you enjoyed the movie and dinner. Do this more often and you won't need me again."

What if I told you that it's none of your business when or where you meet your prince? It doesn't matter if he answers your personal ad, if you meet him at a friend's party, or whether you bump heads with him at a volleyball game. But I can tell you that it will be a pleasant surprise well worth the wait. For now, keep your eyes focused on you and he will come in his own sweet time, in his own sweet way.

An Update on Jane

When last we saw Jane, she'd moved into her parents' house with her son after a nasty divorce from Frog Joe—the one

with the wandering eye who was mean-spirited and unfaithful—
and she started dating Benny, a separated alcoholic co-worker.
Well, fortunately, Jane was growing tired of explaining to her
parents and her friends why she went to so many AA meetings
with him. But the last straw came the day she had to pry her
toddler son's fingers from the bottle of Benny's beer that he'd left
lying on the coffee table. She swiftly dumped him that very evening, and threw herself into her work and mothering. Within a
year she became a regional sales director and moved into a
stunning yet peaceful condo by the beach. She learned French,
Spanish and karate and taught her son to Rollerblade. Another
year passed, and although she'd been in incredible like four
times—six if you count her imaginary affairs with Tom Cruise
and the UPS guy who delivered to her office—still no prince. It's
not that she was looking. Who had the time? But still she felt
an empty spot in her heart that neither her son nor her friends
could fill. So, she took out a personal ad. "Intelligent, fun, cur-
vaceous 36-year-old SWF, looking for passionate, kind, honest,
chivalrous white knight. Usual no's." She also thought about
phoning Benny to see how his recovery was coming. "Nah,"
she thought, "no backsies." Several suitors responded to her
personal ad and she felt hopeful. One at a time, she screened
them over the phone and then in person, if they passed the
phone test. First came Tyrone. A great guy, really, an intellectual
masterpiece, and he had a great butt, but having her dog lap-
ping her face was more satisfying than kissing him. Then Wal-
ter. Funny, with a body builder's physique and almost rich, but
he was about as sensitive as a gorilla. Too much like her tongue-
fu ex-husband. Then Ray, romantic and tender, but utterly underemployed, and always underfoot or speed dialing her day
and night. No goosebumps, no sparks. It was rough out there
in the dating world, but onward she ventured, despite being

convinced that she was the one-date wonder. After some time, and her baby sister's wedding, she questioned what was in store for her. Then one day almost another year later, she was Rollerblading through the park with her son and her dog and she met her prince, who was also Rollerblading through the park with his son and his dog, and now they are all living happily ever after.

Getting Hooked on Having Your Prince in a Hurry

After placing and answering personal ads for a month without so much as one decent prospect, 27-year-old Sheila sunk into a deep depression. Hoping to meet the man of her dreams, 30-year-old Ming launched an enthusiastic prince campaign and frequently scoured the local discos, but when she had not found her beloved at the end of a year, she began dating an old sneaky boyfriend again. I'm not telling you to skip the personal ads or the singles scenes, but drop your insta-prince fantasies. Otherwise, you may wind up feeling the same hurried anxiety as a young child in the backseat of a car on a road trip who keeps asking, "Are we there yet?" You could meet him tomorrow, and then again, you might meet him one year and twelve days from now. Who can say? What I want you to know about finding your prince is that he will appear right there in the middle of your life when you're least expecting it. You do not have to answer 100 personal ads a day, or go to the club every night. If every day you become more of who you want to love by creating a rich, fulfilling life you love, a prince will follow. That is the way it happened for every recovered Frog Princess I've talked to. Here's how they did it.

Secrets of Women Who Found Princes Without Really Looking

1. *They were optimistic.* They kept their visions of their future princes intact without obsessing over them. I did two things to keep my prince vision in the middle of my heart while I was building a life I loved. I wrote him a detailed ten-page letter one day, two years before we met, in present tense, thanking him for being such a wonderful part of my life and talking about all the goodness he'd brought into it, from true friendship, to unspeakable romance, to stepping in as a wise and supportive counselor and second ear for my daughter. The second thing I did was to imagine him tucking me in every night after my meditative prayer sessions. I am almost certain that he was present with me on some level all those months because I had such a vivid picture of him, and I could hear his deep voice bidding me sweet dreams. Some nights I even smelled his scent, which was reminiscent of the ocean. The only thing I couldn't bring into focus was his head, but knowing me, if I could have made out his face, I'd have hired an artist to render him and then a private detective to find him. The more I met with my headless love, the more connected I felt to him, and the more assured I was that we would meet at a time that was best for both of us.

2. *They were at home with themselves.* Dressing up is fun, and who doesn't drool over a new lipstick or mascara? But do you like your precious unmade face? Do you like your body? Your personality? As is and uncensored? Do you delight at your private jokes and eccentric musings? If you are not going to be happy and at home with yourself, then what is the point of being you?

"For a long time, I've had a gardening bug," says 40-year-old Rebecca. "I love to grow things—vegetables, roses, trees. Sometimes I dig around in the garden all day, and when Artis comes home and sees me on my knees with twigs in my hair, he just smiles that 'What else could I expect?' smile and kisses me, dirt and all."

"I know a lot of men like long hair," says Tanya, "but I love my short-short do, and I wouldn't even think about growing it out again. Once a guy told me that I'd look so hot with long hair that he'd date me if I grew it out, and I left him standing there bewildered as I walked off without even responding."

3. *They took good care of themselves.* Any moment—even an ordinary moment—can be turned into an opportunity for indecent indulgence. You don't need a reason, a holiday or a mood to sweep yourself away for an hour (or two) of pampering. Thirty-eight-year-old Malia still gets her hair conditioned and highlighted once a month at the salon where she met Kai, and often has a manicure while she's under the dryer. "It makes me feel special and cared for. It's also one of the things Kai said attracted him to me at first. He loved watching the way I purred when the manicurist massaged the lotion into my hands. If I can't indulge myself, who will? I also like to write myself letters of encouragement and mail them to myself as a reminder of how much I believe in me."

4. *They were approachable.* Forget about simple rejection. One of man's greatest fears is that if he comes over to say something to you he will be repeatedly and irreparably tongue-lanced. If he's a putz, perpetuate this opinion by hissing when he nears you, but if he's got prince potential, lure him over like a snake charmer and keep the conversation spicy. You don't need to read any

more books on flirting or schmoozing. "All you need is a friendly smile," says 23-year-old Karin. "My friends always ask how I meet so many nice guys, and when I tell them my secret is a smile, they think I'm joking."

5. *They were comfortable approaching men who seemed interesting.* "In my book everybody gets one hello, unless they've got 'frog' or 'cretin' plastered on their forehead," says 27-year-old Suzanne. "It's easy, it's quick, and if there's something after the hello, fine. If not, it only took me a few seconds."

"I met my husband at the post office. He was standing in line behind me, thumbing through a copy of *National Geographic* (my favorite magazine), and I wanted to say something to him, and he looked like he wanted to say something to me too. So I asked him to hold my spot while I got a priority mailing label (which I didn't need). When I came back, I thanked him and then he said something corny about the new Bugs Bunny stamps, and then I said something even cornier about the flower series, and then we talked for fifteen minutes about our favorite *National Geographic* spreads until the line went down. Then we exchanged numbers and went out on our first date a few days later," said 27-year-old Ginnie.

6. *They believed in the inherent goodness of men.* If you're a dating field–weary witch with tons of romantic battle scars, then you're not going to recognize a prince if he's right under your nose. Perhaps you have been bruised—okay, almost totaled—by some other men. Do not make innocent men pay for their misdeeds. "I've had a few bad turns. My dad was a jerk. My ex was a jerk. My brother's sort of a jerk. But my best friend has a sweetie pie for a husband, who would kiss the ground she walks on. My cousin's got a good guy too, and he

always treats me with utter respect. I expect to find a good guy too," said 39-year-old Angel.

"I know my prince is out there. I don't care what my girlfriends think," says 22-year-old Penny. "Power to the princes. My boss left work in the middle of the day because his wife was about to go AWOL because their new baby wouldn't stop crying. Later that week he even moved his paternity leave up so he could be at home with the baby while she rested," said 34-year-old Martine.

Once you've mastered the skills above, your chances of attracting a prince will greatly increase, and then, of course, you'll want to go out and practice. Here are seven fun ways to do that.

- ✌ *Network.* According to many career counselors, if you want to find a new job, let everyone know that you're looking. There's no shame in using this strategy to get a new man. Plant seeds. Tell your family, friends, associates, neighbors, etc., that you are looking for prince candidates. Many people have an inner Cupid, so encourage them to keep you on their matchmaking minds. Thirty-two-year-old Jeanne's elderly neighbor asked her to show her visiting grandson their city one summer, and they quickly hit it off and started to date. Doreen, 24, was introduced to her husband by one of her mother's co-workers who heard she was single.
- ✌ *Keep your social calendar full.* If you're like most people, you undoubtedly get several social opportunities a month, from the company picnic to birthday parties. Start accepting them. You never know who might wind up in the seat next to you. "My boss threw an

anniversary party and I ended up spending the whole evening chatting with one of his golf buddies, who turned out to be the most interesting man I've met in years. We made a date for later that week," said 32-year-old Elizabeth. And if you're low on personal invitations, comb through the entertainment section of your local paper and circle a few fun-sounding events to attend.

❧ *Join a singles social group.* If you wanted to find a book, you'd go to a library or a bookstore instead of a supermarket, wouldn't you? If you want to meet more single men, join a singles social group. Look through the Yellow Pages or singles publications, or find out if your church or community center has one. Nowadays many singles groups are activity-based, no seedy, meat-market settings at discos and bars. So you can safely get to know other singles while doing something enjoyable, like taking in a play, sailing, or catching a concert. Laney, 23, says, "I wanted to meet someone and I was sick of personal ads because I'd met too many creeps that way. When I joined a singles club, I remember feeling relieved because I could immediately check for chemistry, which you can't do in an ad. I haven't met Mr. Right yet, but I've met a few nice guys and had a lot of fun."

❧ *Expand your horizons.* Think about things that you like to do, or would like to do, and do more of them. When 40-year-old Elena, who enjoyed listening to jazz, heard her favorite radio station advertise a jazz cruise, without thinking about it too much she picked up the phone and ordered a ticket. She had so much fun she decided to go to a station-sponsored event each month.

❧ *Hang out in coffee shops, parks and other popular spots where people congregate.* Need a cup of Joe to get you going in the morning? "Have it at the nearest Starbucks a few times a week," says 36-year-old Maureen. "That's how I met my boyfriend. It's almost like a social gathering of people in the neighborhood, and it's so easy to start a conversation about—what else?—coffee." If you've got a dog, don't just walk her around the neighborhood, head for a big park where both of you can make new friends.

❧ *Join a hobby club or professional organization.* It's much easier to break the ice with someone you know you've got a few things in common with. Juanita, 28, met her live-in love at a sci-fi convention. "We both came dressed as our favorite *Star Wars* characters and couldn't help but notice each other." Forty-year-old Rose, an attorney, met her boyfriend at a legal convention.

❧ *Go back to school.* If you thumb through a continuing education catalog, you will find loads of interesting, fun classes ranging from home repair to cooking to finance classes. Like hobby and professional organizations, attending lifelong learning class could put you in very close proximity with men you might not otherwise meet who share your interests.

How Will You Know It's Him?

Now that you know you've gotten your negative relationship triggers and fantasies under control, and you have a new and improved set of standards for your prince, I promise you that you'll know when it's him.

Sometimes you will know almost instantly after the infatuation phase passes. Like when you see him do his first dumb thing, and you still think he's seven kinds of wonderful. You'll also feel so comfortable and safe with him whether you are in the best or the worst of times. "When I broke my leg last year my boyfriend asked if he could move in until it healed to take care of me," said 25-year-old Erin. "For weeks, he cooked for me, did my housecleaning, chauffeured me around. Being Miss Independent, I am not the easiest person in the world to nurse, so I was deeply touched by his willingness to work around my ego. I knew he was my prince the night I came hobbling into the front room, barking out orders like a little dictator before I saw he'd fallen asleep on the couch. He woke up, rubbed the sleep from his eyes and said, "Yeah, babe, what do you need?"

When your prince comes calling, it will be hard to miss the fact that he outshines every man you've ever known.

Your Prince Letter

I want you to write a letter to your prince over the next few days, or weeks, or however long it takes. Write it in present tense, and word it as if he's on a trip and you are writing a letter to tell him how grateful you are that he is coming home to you. Before you start writing, imagine all the love and gratitude you'll have to share with him when he finally comes into your life. What will it be like to touch him, to hold him, to kiss him? What will it be like to talk to him, to share ordinary and extraordinary moments with him? Let your imagination soar, engage all of your senses, and do not seal your letter until you have expressed your love completely. Here are some things you might want to consider putting into that letter:

1. Tell him why he was worth the wait.
2. Tell him how he physically excites you.
3. Tell him what it's like to be with someone who exceeds your expectations.
4. Tell him you like the way he treats your friends and family, and your children (if you have them).
5. If you don't have children and want them, tell him why he would be the perfect father for your children.
6. Tell him no man in your past could even hold a candle to him.
7. Tell him you like the way he's honored women in his past.
8. Tell him you feel like God must have spent a little more time on him.
9. Tell him how comfortable you feel with him.
10. Tell him you enjoy how he looks at you.
11. Tell him why you admire him.
12. Tell him about his noble essence.
13. Tell him what you like about his voice and the content of his soul.
14. Tell him how much you enjoy loving someone who shares your hobbies and passions.
15. Tell him what you like about his mind.
16. Tell him what you like about his social skills.
17. Tell him what you like about him spiritually.
18. Tell him what you like about him physically.
19. Tell him why he's a good member of the community and a humanitarian.
20. Tell him how excited you are about sharing the future with him—the trips you'll take, the family you'll raise, the home or shared dreams you'll build together.

When you're finished, seal the letter and put it in the time capsule that you will create during one of the Recovery Exercises at the end of this chapter.

Living Juicy for Two

Last night as my honey leaned against a tree, cradling me in his arms, I thought about all the wonder I've known with this man, and how we continue to expand and deepen as individuals and as a couple. This doesn't mean we don't have our challenges. In many ways, although we are kindred spirits, we are still an experiment in human bonding, and we are very purposeful about protecting this precious thing that we've started. Here are some secrets to keeping your relationship juicy with your future prince.

- ❧ *Cherish him.* If you spend half the amount of time savoring your prince prize as you did getting him, then you'll be off to a good start. Find out what makes him feel appreciated, and when you know, make sure you dedicate a generous amount of time every day letting him know you know he's a prince.
- ❧ *Grow with him.* Just as you bring joy and pleasure to your own life by creating new goals and conquering new frontiers, be visionary about your romantic partnership as well. One couple I know has a monthly marriage goal. Last month they vowed to lose 10 pounds each together (and did). The month before that they realized they'd been eating too much fast food, so they took several cooking classes together, focusing on healthy meals they could prepare in under an hour. Next month,

they are going to tour Europe for thirty days by train, a life-long goal for each.

❖ ***Be best friends.*** Practice demonstrating the kindness and interest in your love that you would extend to any other good friend. "More than I love Artis, I think of him as my best buddy. We go to the movies together. We read books together. We point out things that we know the other would enjoy. We stay up late and talk into the night about nothing and everything," says Rebecca. "The other night I saw a star I hadn't seen before and I dragged him by the hand out to the porch so he could see it too, and he said with the greatest sincerity, 'I'm so glad you came and got me. I wouldn't have wanted to miss that.' " Practice liking each other more.

❖ ***Build your own rituals and experiences together.*** One of the great things about being a couple is that you get to start your own story together and make it something richer than anything you have ever known before. "We both grew up in alcoholic homes, so holidays were either crazy or nonexistent. But after Dennis and I were married, we decided to make up for all the missed holidays by celebrating all of the holidays and our birthdays for three days. And then in addition to that, we've made up our own long holiday, 'TinDen,' which is the twenty-four-day period between my birthday and Dennis's," says 35-year-old Tina. "We exchange little presents every night for twenty-four days, like candies, toys and poems."

❖ ***Define your own relationship.*** Who says you have to publicize your relationship with your prince, or get engaged or marry him the day after you meet him, or even a year or two later? Set your own relationship rhythm and work on preparing to love each other more instead of following anyone else's relationship schedule or ideal. Imhotep and I were at a party once, and someone who knew me but had never met him cornered him for more details after I'd introduced him simply as, "Imhotep." And she asked him what was going on between us, were we dating, engaged—what? He pulled me over, and I answered her question like this, "We are loving each other." That's all you need to say if anyone asks.

⚬ **Let there be spaces in your togetherness.** As Kalil Gibran once said in his treatise on marriage, even in love, you hanker for timeouts from each other. Let there still be spaces for individual hobbies or friends; even a half-hour nap in "your special corner" of the house can be enough of a quality time respite for yourself. Cheyenne, 42, says, "Every other August, I go on a retreat with my girlfriends. Last year we went to Maui for ten days and had the time of our lives. My husband went on a camping trip with his brothers, and when we got back together we shared vacation stories all night in front of the fire and then made mad, passionate love."

⚬ **Find more to love about him.** If you're a parent, you've had the distinct pleasure of being the very first person to love your child, and to watch with utter delight as they reveal themselves a little more to you each day—until they hit those early teen years. Sometimes when we enter adult romantic relationships, we have to remember that our partners are still unfolding, and growing every day, every minute before our very eyes. Or maybe there's something about them that you see every day that you've never really taken the time to salute. Have his eyebrows gotten bushier, or has he sprouted a new gray hair? Is he buffer, rounder, darker? Has his speech pattern

changed? Is he more courageous, more patient, more
funny? Anne Marie, 37, says, "One day I was watching
my husband take our youngest daughter by the hand
to walk her to her bus stop and I heard him call her
'Pumpkin,' for the thousandth time, and I just sat there
with my tea sighing over how lucky I was to have a man
who took the time to see his daughter off to school every
morning and to call her 'Pumpkin.' "

❧ ***Be creative about resolving conflicts.*** Prince Rob
started a marriage diary with his wife Anitra to get them
through ordinary disputes over chores, money, and
the like. In the front of the diary is a statement that they
co-authored that says because they both love and
respect each other and the vows they have taken, they
agree to abide by the spirit of the solutions in their
marriage diary. The way it works is that if one of them
has an issue with something the other has done, they
write it down in the diary, along with the action they
would have preferred instead. Then the other one looks
at the page and signs his or her name in agreement. If,
for any reason, one of them breaks a promise they've
made in the diary, they have to make up for it (and act
like they like it), according to the terms set by their
partner. Rob says, "One night I was so mad at Anitra
about something that I didn't want to sleep in the bed
beside her, but I'd promised her in our diary a long time
ago that I would be in bed every night by eleven (I used
to be a nightowl). I asked her if I could go sleep on the
couch, and she said, 'No, you have to stay. You
promised in our diary.' I knew if I got up, there'd be
consequences, so even though I fumed inside and tossed
and turned a lot, I kept my butt in that bed."

Recovery Exercises

1. Tuck away your prince love letter and any other small items you'd like to give your prince someday in a time capsule.
2. Commit to integrating into your personality one of the methods of finding a prince without really looking, earlier in this chapter.
3. Make a list of places you can go for more opportunities to meet men.

R & R Journal exercise: Make a list of ten things you can do to keep life juicy with your future prince.

Prince David

David, 27, won 27-year-old Melinda's heart at the skating rink, and they've been dating for about a year.

I didn't use to think guys in their 20s were much different than teenage boys, so when I met David at the rink where I often skated, I had already pegged him as a cocky, player type who still had oats to sow and was incapable of having a grown-up relationship. Still, he wasn't bashful about letting me know he was interested. He smiled at me when he rolled past and soon asked me to be his partner in the couples skate, but I didn't bite. His friends laughed at his feeble attempts. One of them, who was also a regular and had tried his stale pickup lines on me before, yelled at David, "Man, you're wasting your time!" It's not that David couldn't have his pick of women. He was by far the best-looking man at the rink, and women seemed to keep cleverly falling down in front of him so he'd have to help them back to their feet.

He accepted my brush-offs gallantly for weeks, and then one afternoon he came over while I was putting my skates on and said, "Is it my breath?" "No," I said trying unsuccessfully to suppress a smile. "I'm just not interested." "Because?" he asked. That's when I shared my theory about the delayed maturity of the male species. He laughed and said he used to feel the same way about 20-something women too, and then he skated off, leaving me sitting there feeling like the dumbest woman on Earth.

But, when it came time for the couples skate, I rolled over to him with my head bowed and my arms folded behind my back and asked him to skate. "I'm still twenty-seven, you know. Are you sure?" he said, starting to laugh. We skated all night, and I came to find out that he was, in fact, a man of substance who had a good job, a semi-normal family and had political leanings similar to mine. I think the thing I like most about him, which was very evident during our early mating dance, is that when we have a disagreement, he doesn't just stomp off like most of the guys I've dated or bully me until I give in. He really tries to understand what I'm feeling, and communicate what he's feeling in a positive way, even if it's hard. One of his favorite ways of starting into a touchy subject is by saying, "I don't know if this is going to come out right, and we can work that out after I say it, but here goes. . . ."

STEP 11

Celebrate Your Milestones

Lesson: Every step you take to build a healthier relationship with yourself so you can live juicy and choose a prince the next time is a reason to celebrate. Baby steps, big steps— acknowledge them all!

Affirmations

1. I'm getting better and better every day.
2. I celebrate what I've gained and what I've released.
3. I'm proud of myself, right now.

Very early one morning as the sun rose over the beach, Nikki started to build a sand castle. She put all of her concentration into the castle, sculpting it quietly, without rest, until she became oblivious even to the sounds of the children playing around her on the now crowded beach. After some time, a group of people walked by and admiringly said, "You are so talented. You must be proud."

"Not yet," said Nikki. "I still have to add another wing."

Soon after she'd added another wing, a woman came by and said, "My, what a lovely castle."

"Not yet," said Nikki. "I haven't added the windows."

Soon after she'd added the windows, a man came by with a camera and said, "Wow, what an amazing sand castle. This is a thousand times more wonderful than my girlfriend described it. May I take a picture?"

"Not yet, I haven't added the doors," said Nikki, who'd been working for hours and hours straight.

Eventually Nikki had to take a potty break. She stood up and looked at her work, without even the slightest trace of pride in the masterpiece before her. "I'll have to add more detail when I get back," she thought before heading off.

She had taken no more than a few steps from it when suddenly there was a loud roar of thunder, followed by a heavy rainstorm that quickly washed her sand castle away.

Often in the rush to get to where we *think* we should be, like Nikki, we do not take enough time to fully caress what we are creating each and every moment. When was the last time you stopped to taste the fruits of all of your toiling and earnest effort to re-create your love life?

Eliminate Your Guilt About Living Celebrations

I have a confession to make. I used to be celebration-impaired. Somehow, somewhere I slipped into constant conquest mode, and was often too hung up on perfection or what came next to do anything other than mechanically check off an accomplishment. I ran God knows how many miles every day for over two decades, pushing for more aerobic speed and endurance, totally oblivious to the fact that someone once celebrated my first mastery of gravity, and clapped for me when I took my first wobbly steps. And when I spoke before a TV audience for the first time, I forgot that someone had squealed with delight over my first baby gibberish sentence.

I regret to tell you that I didn't celebrate my divorce until years later either. I didn't celebrate the first time I hung up on a frog or the last time I plucked petals off some poor, unsuspecting daisy while reciting, "All men should be beamed off of the planet, all men should be beamed off of the planet not."

And I should have. I should have stopped everything and launched into a *Flashdance What A Feeling* victory dance.

Even now, I remember my first frog-recovery diva dance after dumping a man after only two dates. We were on a second date hike and as we rested on a log at the bottom of the trail, he reached over and pinched the back of one of my thighs and said I had good muscle tone; that usually women over thirty had cottage cheese thighs. Up until this moment I thought he was an intelligent, interesting man and was looking forward to a third date, but after I passed his "test," I canceled our next date, dropped him off without another word, and went home to somersault across my lawn.

Don't miss out. Celebrate all of your wins, every last one. You deserve it. And the more you do it, the easier it will become. If you feel guilty about stomping out a victory dance, somersaulting across your lawn hooting and hollering or doing anything else that for you says "I've won!" then take this moment to get a slip of paper and write yourself a permission slip.

From this moment forward, I _____ *(your name)* can celebrate all of the sweet victories in my life, big and small, with gusto because I said so.

The Key to Celebrating All the Time

It's the celebration-impaired recovering frog princess's nightmare: you're on the road to princes, and some enthusiastic little cheerleader (that would be me) insists that you break out the vino and candles to toast something—anything—that you've done to repair your love life, and you can't think of a thing. Now what?

Take a deep breath, and hear me out. You have at least twenty-five things to pat yourself on the back for at this very moment. All you have to do to fill up your "brag sheet" list right now is change your criteria for celebrations. An older friend once told me that his criteria for happiness was that he woke up every day. That's his entire reason for looking like Pollyanna's big brother.

But if you're anything like the average recovering frog princess, your celebratory bar is set way too high and you're undoubtedly missing out on some juicy, juicy victory parties. I bet you probably still think in the back of your mind that you're not worth the wine because you don't have the prince you want yet. So, let's work on that notion for a bit. In fact, I'll spot you seven reasons to throw a mini-party today.

1. You're reading this page.
2. You've read every page before it.
3. You repeated the affirmations at the beginning of this step.
4. You wrote yourself a permission-to-celebrate slip.
5. You've kept your No More Frogs Pledge for three days. (Remember the Rewards of Being a Good Girl treat chart, pp. 62–63, back in Step 3.)
6. You've kept your No More Frogs Pledge for a week.
7. You're you.

It might even help to put your inner child in charge of the accolades. She'll know what to do. Yesterday, a small girl who appeared to be about 4 years old was tumbling and twirling around while her mother stood in line before me, and boom, she fell down. Just as she was looking around for some sympathy and scrunching up her lip to pout, her mother said, "Guess what, Kimmie? Let's see how fast my good girl can get back up." Kimmie scrambled back up in two seconds, giggling, and proud as punch of herself she pronounced, "I'm a good girl!" and started tumbling around again. You can do that too, you know?

After you've begun to cozy up to this idea of bouncing back and embracing all of the resilience and magic that is within you, you'll find you can go from one celebration to the next with that same childlike glee.

As you come up with your list of reasons to celebrate right now, record them in your R & R Journal. If you get stuck before you get to twenty-five, here are some things to keep in mind:

1. What's the best thing that's happened to your mind without frogs?
2. What's the best thing that's happened to your heart without frogs?
3. What's the best thing that's happened to your body without frogs?
4. What's the best thing that's happened to your spirit without frogs?
5. What have you gained without frogs in your life?
6. What have you released that no longer serves you?
7. Who has come into your life since you've made healthier love choices, and what value have they added to your life?
8. What unexpected problems have you conquered?
9. What's been the best part of your recovery effort?

10. How have you become a better you?
11. What "firsts" can you celebrate? Consider these:
    - 🐸 The first moment you decided you didn't want to be a Frog Princess anymore.
    - 🐸 The first time you forgave yourself for choosing a frog in the past.
    - 🐸 Your first prince sighting.
    - 🐸 The first time you were able to identify one of the seven common frog species.
    - 🐸 The first time you knew right away that you weren't going to die after you broke up with someone you thought you loved who wasn't right for you.
    - 🐸 The first time you called on your frog recovery sponsor.
    - 🐸 The first time you spent quality time with yourself in the middle of your otherwise busy life.
12. What "lasts" can you celebrate?
    - 🐸 The last time you gave your phone number to, kissed, touched or slept with a man who was beneath your standards.
    - 🐸 The last time you pretended to be someone else to please a man.
    - 🐸 The last time you went to a frog metropolis.
    - 🐸 The last time you looked at a picture of an old love and sighed.
    - 🐸 The last time you kept his memory alive by talking about him as if he were the best thing since sliced bread.
    - 🐸 The last time you beat yourself up for past relationship drama.
    - 🐸 The last time you let a frog talk you down when you were breaking up with him.

❧ The last time you thought you were too _____ to have a prince.

Ten Sure Signs You Don't Have a Frog Habit Anymore

I want you to bookmark this page, and fill out the questionnaire below in a month. If it looks suspiciously familiar, that's because it's a modified version of the one you took in the beginning of this book, only this time it's designed to bring out the good in you by showing you how far you've come, baby.

- ❑ I feel complete without a man or a relationship so I take my time partnering and quickly chuck bad relationships.
- ❑ I don't date jerks anymore because they're cute, successful, totally infatuated with me, or better than nothing.
- ❑ I don't hesitate to repel frog-like men.
- ❑ I don't feel bad, stupid, or disappointed in myself after hooking up with the new men in my life.
- ❑ I spend a lot of earnest time on a date sizing a man up.
- ❑ According to my closest friends, my last love interest was a quality man.
- ❑ When I tell my female friends about my dates they are hopeful for all of womankind.
- ❑ My love life is both practical and passionate, and I'm a good role model for young girls who believe in love.
- ❑ I'm more likely to praise myself for being too picky when I know the guy I'm seeing is a loser, and to dump him.
- ❑ If I knew a man was certifiably a frog and he called right now and asked me out, I'd hang up on him and block his phone number.

The more items you checked, the better your frog recovery is going and the more reasons you'll have to celebrate.

Another thing we touched on in the beginning was the Frog Catcher's Hall of Shame. Remember the twelve women I used to scare you straight, so you'd never fiddle with a frog again? Well, it's time for your walk through the Queen's Hall of Glory now, so you can celebrate in spirit with the women who have crossed over.

Queen's Hall of Glory

- ✒ *Nattalie, 29, artist.* "My ex-husband, who I confess I used to still have sex with every now and then, called the other night to see if he could come over, and I told him I had to paint my toenails and hung up."
- ✒ *Bonita, 31, dental hygienist.* "This dentist was romantically interested in me, but he had the personality of a fly. I kept putting him off, and one day as the big pitch he offered to take me to Paris for a week. Man, that's one of the places I dream about. And I'll get there one day, but definitely not with him."
- ✒ *Rita, 22, personal trainer.* "It's been three months since I moved out and away from my boyfriend. I miss him, even though he thought marijuana was an acceptable in-between-meals snack. But I'm not freaking out anymore. I'm also not thinking about calling him to see if he misses me too. I guess the truth is that I don't care anymore what he thinks."
- ✒ *Whitney, 43, executive.* "My ex-husband was such a jealous jerk that I used to dress in baggy clothes so men wouldn't look at me and set him off. Well, last week I splurged on a brand new form-fitting wardrobe. Hell, I look good, why can't I flaunt it?"

❧ **Beth, 36, pharmacist.** "I used to shut myself off from my friends, who are such a wonderful source of comfort after a breakup, but now we have pampering nights and give each other facials, massages and pedicures."

❧ **Carrie, 30, event planner.** "Before my ex left me for another woman, he was the only thing standing between me and a promotion in a new city I loved. Fortunately the transfer opportunity came up again and I went. It's the best move I've ever made."

❧ **Beryl, 34, mother.** "I have been happy all week. I can't remember the last time I had such a pleasant week. No worries about what kind of mood my ex husband would be in, what I had forgotten to do to keep him happy, or him just being frustrated at me for no good reason. I know that there will be some ugly times ahead with getting back on my feet again after I leave the shelter, but I feel like I'm getting a second chance at life, and so are my children."

Recovery Exercises

1. Schedule a regular recap and celebration time each day.
2. How many of the items on the Ten Sure Signs You Don't Have a Frog Habit Anymore list can you check off today?

R & R Journal exercise: Make a list of ten things you can celebrate today, and celebrate them.

Prince Artis

Artis is a 42-year-old computer programmer who works fifty-plus hours a week so Rebecca, 40, his wife of fourteen years, can stay home to raise their 5- and 7-year-old sons. She tells this story:

When we met at a carnival over fifteen years ago, I was a little suspicious of Artis's friendly small talk because I had just ended a two-year relationship with a verbally abusive man who had also been sweet at first. Somehow Artis sensed my past hurt, and backed off. But for the next hour, wherever I went, he magically appeared in line before me. Finally he turned around in the cotton candy line one time, smiled and said, "I'm a scientist and I wondered if you could help me test a theory. Let's plan to show up at the same place for the next hour and see if we can beat our unplanned record."

We never got to test the experiment because we both started laughing and that broke the ice, and we were inseparable for the rest of the day.

Every day for the last fourteen years he has been that same nice, funny, thoughtful, genuine guy I met at the carnival—to me and to our boys, who adore him. He's their little league soccer coach too.

I guess I just love the way he loves me. Not a week goes by without some symbol of his love secretly planted around the house—flowers, cards, or something he knows would please me. The cards always make me cry. Last week's said, "Every day I thank God for giving me the greatest treasure in the world. You."

Prince Artis was born with one leg.

STEP 12

Remember

Lesson: The road to mastery is paved with good reminders and repetition.

Affirmations

1. I love reviewing new skills until I perfect them.
2. My memory of healthy habits is very long.
3. Mastery is mine.

Here are some reminders to help you stay on the path to relationship riches.

Q. *What is a frog?*

A. A frog is a slimy amphibian that you had to dissect in biology class around eighth grade unless you fainted or had a really good protest note from your parents. A frog is also a man who **f**ails the **r**equirements **of g**reatness.

They invoke grief, trauma and heartbreak, and therefore should not be talked to, touched, kissed, bedded or married by any woman looking for a healthy romantic partnership. (page 16)

Q. *If they are so gross, how can they become so habit forming?*

A. Most of the time they are cute, rich, charming, and hypnotic, or you are desperate, lonely, in denial, have grand Ms. Fix-It delusions, or do not know the difference between a good man who's having a bad moment and a green-blooded frog. (pages 18–21)

Q. *What is Frog mind?*

A. It is a state of thinking that puts you at risk for any of the momentary psychological disorders described above. (page 38)

Q. *What is a prince?*

A. A man who can **p**rovide **r**omance, **i**nspiration, **n**urturing, and **c**haracter **e**asily and who **p**revents **r**ecurring **i**diotic **n**egative **c**razy **e**xperiences with frogs. (pages 3–4)

Q. *How can I prepare myself to meet a prince?*

A. Follow this formula: Self-love^n − frogs and bad mating habits + healthy partnering strategies = happily ever after (page 4)

Q. *Can I date frogs during my recovery?*

A. Consider this a frog fast. No frogs for breakfast, lunch or dinner. No frogs, period. (page 33)

Q. *What are the three steps I should take to resolve negative feelings about old frogs and the former me who chose them?*

A. (1) Forgive. (2) Release. (3) Replenish. (pages 32–33)

Q. *Excuse me, but why would I want to forgive a frog?*

A. For entirely selfish reasons. It will help you heal your heart wounds, and make *yourself* stronger and better. Once you forgive, it will be easier to release frogs and the pieces of your heart and your soul that you've leased out to frogs will come flooding back to you. Trust, me, it'll be one of your best magic tricks. (page 32)

Q. *What is a negative mating trigger and why should I be wary of them?*

A. A negative mating trigger is any seemingly small but mortal temptation that can suddenly impair your rational mating sensibilities, making you a prime candidate for Frog mind. (page 42)

Q. *What are the five common negative mating triggers?*

A. (1) Physical attraction. (2) Negative emotional states. (3) Peer pressure. (4) Lust. (5) A man's wallet size. (pages 43–47)

Q. *How can I conquer negative triggers?*

A. Study your weaknesses and come up with antidotes. Also, plan ahead when you know you're going to be in frog territory or internally vulnerable. And lastly, pay attention to what your core needs are, and when you feel a trigger coming on, pinpoint a healthy desire that could satisfy you. (pages 51–52)

Q. How can I motivate myself to change my froggy ways?

A. Use carrots (positive rewards) or sticks (negative consequences) to keep yourself on the prince path. For example, reward yourself for squashing one of your negative
triggers with a pampering treat or visualize the new
peace ahead when you're totally frog-free. Or keep yourself on track by thinking of the pain or shame you will
feel if a year from now you are still a Frog Princess.
(pages 58–59)

Q. What should I do if I get in a motivational slump?

A. Pray, play, pamper and push through. It might also help
just to hang out and review your carrot and stick motivations and wait for your juice to return. (pages 70–71)

Q. What are the four things I need to do to live juicy?

A. (1) Be at home with yourself. (2) Build a dream. (3) Ignite
your pampering flame. (4) Spend quality time with yourself. (pages 77–84)

*Q. I have a hectic life, I have children—how do I find the
time to pamper myself?*

A. Slow down and make the time. Your children will survive
without you while you're enjoying a candlelit bubble bath
for twenty minutes. Also, know what makes you feel pampered, budget it in, pencil it in if you have to and savor it.
(pages 85–87)

Q. What are the top three breakup challenges?

A. (1) You're still expecting a miracle. (2) You don't know how
to end it. (3) You're scared he'll raise a stink. (page 92)

Q. *What's the best way to manage them?*

A. By permanently installing the right breakup attitude, which goes as follows: *I want to break up with him for good today no matter what he says or does because he is a frog and I deserve better.* (pages 92–93)

Q. *Why should I initiate a sex moratorium shortly before a breakup?*

A. If you have sex with anyone you're about to break up with, it will only cloud the issue and send mixed messages. (page 93)

Q. *What if I don't feel strong enough to stay away from a frog I've broken up with but still have the hots for?*

A. Call your frog recovery sponsor, and allow her to talk you down. (pages 94–95)

Q. *What are the important things to remember during the breakup speech?*

A. ✦ *Be focused and clear.* It will keep you in control of the conversation.

  ✦ *Do not say anything that breeds confusion* or leaves room for makeup work or repair, like "Let's be friends" or "Maybe I just need a little space right now."

  ✦ *Do not let him talk to you after your normal bedtime,* or when you're bone tired, or allow him to go on for hours about the same thing. It's downright hypnotic.

  ✦ *Avoid physical contact.* No goodbye kisses, hugs or handholding.

⮢ **Decide on a threshold for begging, whining and appeals.** When you've had enough, go. You do not have to stay until he agrees to let go of you. (page 97)

Q. *What are seven common species of frogs?*
A. (1) Brute. (2) Boy-Boy. (3) Sneaky. (4) High-N-Low. (5) Fossil. (6) Icy. (7) Mismatch. (pages 100–107)

Q. *When is it okay to call a frog after you've broken up with him?*
A. Never. Don't call to ask for your things back. Don't call to tell him to stop calling you. Don't call to tell him he's a jerk. (page 110)

Q. *After I dump a frog, how else do I purge?*
A. Get rid of *all* things that remind you of him—clothing, letters, pictures, furniture and knickknacks. (pages 113–14)

Q. *How can I break up with someone who might be violent?*
A. You can break up by letter, by phone and by proxy. And if you fear for your physical safety afterward, look into getting a restraining order. (page 100)

Q. *How can I ward off frogs in the future?*
A. (1) Body repelling. (2) Tongue repelling. (3) Psychic repelling. Say the thing you think he least wants to hear, while positioning your body as if you're ready to flee and set up a general psychic net that will keep him away from you. (pages 122–24)

Q. *Is it acceptable to run if I see a jerk headed my way in a public place?*

A. Yes. Always wear comfortable shoes, because, well, you just never know when you'll have to break into a jog. (page 122)

Q. *How do I start raising my standards for men?*

A. *First,* you need to know what "better" is. *Second,* you need to really believe you deserve "better." *Third,* you need to globally integrate your new belief into your lifestyle. Start with smaller things like taking more time to pick better produce at the grocery store and buying quality clothing, and soon you will also become a connoisseur of good men. (page 135)

Q. *What are some basic things that I should look for in a prince?*

A. (1) Monogamy. (2) Character and integrity. (3) Kindness. (4) Romance. (5) Good health. (6) Emotional support. (7) Maturity. (8) Sobriety. (page 137)

Q. *What if the prince I find happens to be a recovering frog?*

A. Friend, maybe. Romantic partner? Nah. Wait until he's fully recovered. Then, and only then, will he qualify to be your prince. (page 107)

Q. *Is it okay to have two sets of standards for men— those I will have sex with and those I want a healthy long-term relationship with?*

A. What would make you want to share your precious body with a frog? (page 145)

Q. *What's wrong with sex with a frog if it's fun?*

A. (1) It could lead to a false sense of emotional connection that would prevent you from dumping him, (2) pregnancy, or (3) STDs. (page 171)

Q. *What's the single most important thing to do on a date with a new guy?*

A. Pay attention to who he really is and whether that measures up to your standards. (page 150)

Q. *What's the best way to figure out if a guy meets my standards?*

A. Date in daylight, don't overdress or overprepare, use all of your senses to evaluate him, and bury your expectations. A date is just a date. It doesn't have to lead to a kiss, sex, a long-term relationship, marriage, or even another date. (pages 151–52)

Q. *How do I get my sexual groove going while I'm waiting for my prince?*

A. Here are six passion breaks for one that should keep you pretty euphoric. (1) Masturbate. (2) Learn to be more sensual in nonsexual ways. (3) Indulge in virtual sex with a hot fantasy partner. (4) Watch a sexually explicit movie. (5) Take up a sexy hobby. (6) Buy sexy lingerie or clothing. (pages 172–74)

Q. *How do I manage my emotions during my recovery?*

A. Journal, repeat positive affirmations, pray, and exercise. (page 176)

Q. *What do I do until I find my prince?*

A. Enjoy being you and strive every day to create a life you love even more. (page 184)

Q. *How do I find my prince once I've gotten rid of the frogs and become emotionally healthy?*

A. (1) Remain optimistic. (2) Be at home with yourself. (3) Take good care of yourself. (4) Be approachable. (5) Be comfortable approaching men who seem suitable and interesting. (6) Believe in the inherent goodness of men. (pages 185–88)

Q. *How will I know it's him?*

A. Now that you've gotten your negative relationship triggers and fantasies under control, and you have a new and improved set of standards for your prince, I promise you that you'll know when it's him. (pages 190–91)

Q. *What do I do after I find him?*

A. Keep it juicy. Cherish him, grow with him, be his best friend, build your own rituals and experiences together, give each other space, find more to love about him, be creative about resolving conflicts, and celebrate, celebrate, celebrate! (pages 193–96)

Recovery Exercises

1. Once you've recovered from your frog addiction, remember to revisit step 12 for a refresher now and again.
2. Share what you've learned so far with someone who needs it too.

R & R Journal exercise: Write yourself and your frog recovery sponsor thank-you letters for taking such a big step to not talk to, touch, marry or otherwise fiddle with another frog.

Prince Imhotep

I met Imhotep three years ago at a bookstore, and have been loving him madly ever since on so many levels. He is an incredible friend, lover, creative co-conspirator and a spiritual partner. He is also the funniest man alive.

An acquaintance introduced me to his friend Imhotep, and I looked up into a pair of eyes that simultaneously held a look of childish wonder and sage-like wisdom. And yet, even with his long mane of luscious dreads that glistened with silver and brown sugar my first thought was not, "Hallelujah, he has come!" Still I had a feeling it was one of those divine meetings that come maybe once in a lifetime—if you're lucky.

We had a brief friendly chat, not unlike one any two book lovers might have had in a bookstore, and I didn't see him again until a year later, in front of a natural food co-op. As I crossed the street, I felt a kind of "quickening" before I spotted him, a lot like the excitement I feel when the circus is coming to town. Shamelessly enough, I was on my way for a massage with another man I had the hots for, and was simply stopping by the co-op to pick up some carrot juice.

I'd forgotten Imhotep's name, but those shining eyes I remembered. We exchanged numbers this time, and I hurried off to meet massage boy. But Imhotep and I became fast friends, often calling each other to talk for hours about metaphysics, spirituality, and sometimes, just to laugh. Often after an hour or so on the phone, I felt like we'd gone on a long, rich journey together, and to have to get off the phone and do something ordinary like load the dryer was a little deflating.

I don't know how it happened exactly but months later—after I told Imhotep we should remain friends, mind you—I looked at him one day, and he looked at me and in that instant we both saw our future.

Every time I'm with him I am absolutely certain that the sweetest days can follow the darkest nights, that princes follow frogs.

More than almost anything else, I love seven things about him: (1) He's the most gracious man I know; (2) He's a creative light, both through his artwork, his cooking and his storytelling; (3) He loves his children and he's a good friend to them as well as a father, and (4) he's extended that love to my daughter Esprit; (5) He regards his body as a temple and takes the best care of it; (6) He is the funniest man alive; (7) He always looks at and treats me like I have hung the moon.

And every single laugh and lesson in this book is my tribute to him.

Last Words

I want to leave you with a thought before I go. I have loved writing this book knowing that one day you'd pick it up and I'd be your guide through your exciting journey to becoming a healthier person to love while finding someone healthy to love. Many nights I fell asleep with a pen in my hand, tired to the bone, and yet, still believed that there'd be something I'd have to wake up and tell you around 2 A.M. Know that you've been with me in spirit this whole time, in every word, in every laugh, and that it is my hope of hopes that you've gotten what you needed to live a juicier, richer life, with prince or without.

If I were there with you now we'd sit down and laugh about all the craziness we've both created in our love lives up until this point. For me it's all come full circle now, and I realize that without the frogs of my past, I would never have been able to give you this blueprint to do better, and that, my friend, is a blessing in my life that I cannot express in words.

APPENDIX

Ninety-nine Recovery & Rapture Journal Ideas

In addition to the R & R exercises throughout the book, invest at least fifteen minutes more each day for the next month writing in your journal on one of the topics below. I promise you, it will be an exciting, educational journey that will help you to be more in touch with yourself, celebrate yourself, and love yourself, so don't skimp. You'll be amazed at what comes out of you, and through you. Each of the mini self-portraits you create will help you to grow the new life you want. Who knows, maybe you'll even decide to share them one day with your future prince.

1. Write about your favorite day.
2. Write about the thing you're most proud of.
3. Write about your favorite childhood toy.
4. Write about a color you like and why it's your favorite, and when you discovered it was.
5. Write about another name you'd choose.

6. Write about the one moment in future time you'd like to have revealed to you.
7. Write ten things you would do if no one knew.
8. Write about something you're embarrassed about.
9. Write about something you're proud of.
10. Write about something that scares you.
11. Write about something you did for the last time without knowing it was the last time.
12. Write about your last random act of kindness.
13. Write about someone else's last random act of kindness toward you.
14. Write about your favorite gift from someone, and how you came to love it.
15. Write about what you'd do for a living if you were still ten years old.
16. Write about the first time you had sex.
17. Write about the last time you had sex.
18. Write about the things that please you.
19. Write about a something that surprised you today.
20. Write about how you're feeling about writing today.
21. Write about a friend's husband or boyfriend that you think is perfect.
22. Write about the kind of mate you wish for your daughter, best friend or sisters.
23. Write about your favorite hobby.
24. Write about the three biggest things you want to do in your lifetime.
25. Write about how you'd get out of a bad relationship if you were someone else.
26. Write about why your best friend in elementary school was your best friend.
27. Write about your first love.

28. Write about the way you were before you discovered boys.
29. Write about why your best friend in high school was your best friend.
30. Write about why your current best friend is your best friend.
31. Write about a woman you admire.
32. Write about a man you admire.
33. Write about a child you admire.
34. Write about the most interesting thing you saw on TV last year.
35. Write about what it would be like to be without TV or radio for a year.
36. Write about the three people you would want to be stranded with on a desert island.
37. Write about getting lost in a strange place, and discovering something wonderful while you were there.
38. Write about a scent you love and how it makes you feel when you smell it.
39. Write about three predictions you have for the next decade.
40. Write about your favorite song.
41. Write about who you'd be if you weren't you.
42. Write about something you wish you could do over.
43. Write about something you'd never do over.
44. Write about the best thing that ever happened to you after the worst thing that ever happened to you.
45. Write a theme song for yourself.
46. Write a self-portrait poem.
47. Write your autobiography.
48. Write about how you'd like to be remembered.
49. Write about how much you're like your mother.
50. Write about how you're not like your mother.

51. Write about how the men in your life are like your father.
52. Write about how the men in your life aren't like your father.
53. Write about the things you're most afraid of seeing in yourself.
54. Write about a time when you had more faith than you knew what to do with.
55. Write about your favorite season.
56. Write about your least favorite season.
57. Write about one area of your life where your standards are exceptionally high.
58. Write about the TV show you'd star in.
59. Write about the last promise you made to yourself.
60. Write about a promise you wish you could make to yourself and keep.
61. Write the names of five people you love and explain why you love them.
62. Write the words you want on your headstone.
63. Write about your biggest dream.
64. Write about your biggest celebration.
65. Write about an imaginary boyfriend.
66. Write about the wisest person you know.
67. Write about what you'd ask a genie if you had three wishes.
68. Write about the hardest thing you've ever done.
69. Write about your mission.
70. Write about the last dream you remember.
71. Write about your favorite daydream.
72. Write about your perfect wedding ceremony.
73. Write about the last thing you let go of.
74. Write about a time when you took an unpopular stance.
75. Write about the last cause you championed.

76. Write about a cause you want to champion.
77. Write about willpower.
78. Write ten predictions for your coming year.
79. Write about another period in time you'd like to visit.
80. Write about the best thing about living in this time.
81. Write about all the things you like to do alone.
82. Write about something you need another person to do.
83. Write about a time you've been in love.
84. Write about a time you've been in deep like.
85. Write about a time someone has loved you and you didn't love them back.
86. Write about your favorite piece of furniture.
87. Write about your favorite place in the world.
88. Write about five things you want to do in the next year.
89. Write about your shadow.
90. Write about the last thing that made you cry.
91. Write about getting your period for the first time.
92. Write about your sexual fantasy.
93. Write a letter to your younger self.
94. Write about the last time you were assertive.
95. Write about your last celebration.
96. Write about what you'd do if you hit the lottery.
97. Write a forgiveness letter to the person who has hurt you the most.
98. Write a gratitude letter to the person who has loved you the best.
99. Write about what you think Robert Browning meant when he wrote, "Grow old with me, the best is yet to be."

ACKNOWLEDGMENTS

To my daughter, Esprit, may you find a prince the first time. Thank you for being so patient with me, I know it's not always easy to have a mom who's not like all the rest. *I do.* Maybe when you hit your twenties, I'll seem more normal, but I hope not. Thanks too for putting up with my shushing you while I was writing, although you didn't half of the time, and sharing your health handouts for Step 9. Yes, it's one of those "empowerment" books again. Maybe next time, I'll write a mystery novel just for you.

To Alma, sister friend divine, thank you for minimizing our phone chats and "sister time" so I could hole up and write again. I owe you at least two dozen phone calls and who knows how many spa days, don't I?

Thanks to all the women who opened their love lives to me— the good, bad and the ugly—so I could share truth, lessons and a healing prescription with other women who needed to know.

To the cast of *Star Trek: Voyager,* another great season. I cherished your weekly doses of extraterrestrial resuscitation more than I can ever say.

To Janis Donnaud, my agent, for taking care of the business details so I could do two of the things I most love to do, write and dream.

To everyone at Plume—especially to my gifted editor, Amanda Patten—for transporting this manuscript into a finished book.

To God, for blessing me with another opportunity to share an inspirational, healing, and hopeful message, which, now that it's all written and done, has been as much a gift to me as anyone.